FAST TRACK TO SUCCESS

SALES

FAST TRACK TO SUCCESS
SALES

JOHN MACTEAR

Prentice Hall
FINANCIAL TIMES

An imprint of **Pearson Education**
Harlow, England • London • New York • Boston • San Francisco • Toronto • Sydney • Singapore • Hong Kong
Tokyo • Seoul • Taipei • New Delhi • Cape Town • Madrid • Mexico City • Amsterdam • Munich • Paris • Milan

PEARSON EDUCATION LIMITED

Edinburgh Gate
Harlow CM20 2JE
Tel: +44 (0)1279 623623
Fax: +44 (0)1279 431059
Website: www.pearsoned.co.uk

First published in Great Britain in 2009

ISBN: 978-0-273-72176-5

British Library Cataloguing-in-Publication Data
A catalogue record for this book is available from the British Library

Library of Congress Cataloging-in-Publication Data
Mactear, John.
  Fast track to success : sales / John Mactear.
      p. cm.-- (Fast track series)
  Includes bibliographical references and index.
  ISBN 978-0-273-72176-5 (pbk. : alk. paper) 1. Sales management. I. Title. II. Title: Sales.
  HF5438.4.M33 2009
  658.8'1--dc22
                            2009005447

10 9 8 7 6 5 4 3 2 1
13 12 11 10 09

Series text design by Design Deluxe
Typeset in 10/15 Swis Lt by 30
Printed by Ashford Colour Press Ltd., Gosport

The publisher's policy is to use paper manufactured from sustainable forests.

CONTENTS

THE FAST TRACK WAY

Everything you need to accelerate your career

The best way to fast track your career as a manager is to fast track the contribution you and your team make to your organisation and for your team to be successful in as public a way as possible. That's what the Fast Track series is about. The Fast Track manager delivers against performance expectations, is personally highly effective and efficient, develops the full potential of their team, is recognised as a key opinion leader in the business, and ultimately progresses up the organisation ahead of their peers.

You will benefit from the books in the Fast Track series whether you are an ambitious first-time team leader or a more experienced manager that is keen to develop further over the next few years. You may be a specialist aiming to master every aspect of your chosen discipline or function, or simply be trying to broaden your awareness of other key management disciplines and skills. In either case, you will have the motivation to critically review yourself and your team using the tools and techniques presented in this book, as well as the time to stop, think and act on areas you identify for improvement.

Do you know what you need to know and do to make a real difference to your performance at work, your contribution to your company and your blossoming career? For most of us, the honest answer is 'Not really, no'. It's not surprising then that most of us never reach our full potential. The innovative Fast Track series gives you exactly what you need to speed up your progress and become a high performance manager in all the areas of the business that matter. Fast Track is not just another 'How to' series. Books on selling tell you how to win sales but not how to move from salesperson to sales manager. Project management software enables you to plan detailed tasks but doesn't improve the quality of your project management thinking and business performance. A marketing book tells you about the principles of marketing but not how to lead a team of marketers. It's not enough.

Specially designed features in the Fast Track books will help you to see what you need to know and to develop the skills you need to be successful. They give you:

→ the information required for you to shine in your chosen function or skill – particularly in the Fast Track top ten;

→ practical advice in the form of Quick Tips and answers to FAQs from people who have been there before you and succeeded;

→ state of the art best practice as explained by today's academics and industry experts in specially written Expert Voices;

→ case stories and examples of what works and, perhaps more importantly, what doesn't work;

→ comprehensive tools for accelerating the effectiveness and performance of your team;

→ a framework that helps you to develop your career as well as produce terrific results.

Fast Track is a resource of business thinking, approaches and techniques presented in a variety of ways – in short, a complete performance support environment. It enables managers to build careers from their first tentative steps into management all the way up to becoming a business director – accelerating the performance of their team and their career. When you use the Fast Track approach with your team it provides a common business language and structure, based on best business practice. You will benefit from the book whether or not others in the organisation adopt the same practices; indeed if they don't, it will give you an edge over them. Each Fast Track book blends hard practical advice from expert practitioners with insights and the latest thinking from experts from leading business schools.

The Fast Track approach will be valuable to team leaders and managers from all industry sectors and functional areas. It is for ambitious people who have already acquired some team leadership skills and have realised just how much more there is to know.

If you want to progress further you will be directed towards additional learning and development resources via an interactive Fast Track website, **www.Fast-Track-Me.com**. For many, these books therefore become the first step in a journey of continuous development. So, the Fast Track approach gives you everything you need to accelerate your career, offering you the opportunity to develop your knowledge and skills, improve your team's performance, benefit your organisation's progress towards its aims and light the fuse under your true career potential.

ABOUT THE AUTHOR

JOHN MACTEAR is a senior management consultant with Mercuri International, one of the world's largest sales consultancies. At Mercuri he is actively involved with selling as well as developing and delivering sales and sales management training workshops to companies across all industries around the world. He has 25 years' experience in selling to small and medium-sized enterprises as well as the world's largest multi-nationals in Europe, North America and the Middle and Near East.

Having lived in North America for over ten years, he brings the best in sales techniques from both sides of the Atlantic. He has worked in front-line sales, led international sales teams and inspired third party distributors. John has also run international business redesign projects and has spent over five years in marketing director roles. He gained a BSc at Southampton University in 1981.

E john@mactear.com
T 00 44 (0) 777 307 33 704

A WORD OF THANKS FROM THE AUTHOR

I would like to thank the following for their generous contributions to this book.

→ **Liz Gooster, Pearson**. There are many exciting new ideas in the publishing world at present, but without an enthusiastic champion, most will simply die a slow death. Liz had the confidence to commission the Fast Track series and associated web-tool on behalf of the Pearson Group at a time when other publishers were cutting back on non-core activities. She has remained committed to its success – providing direction, challenge and encouragement as and when required.

→ **Ken Langdon**. As well as being a leading author in his own right, Ken has worked with all the Fast Track authors to bring a degree of rigour and consistency to the series. As each book has developed, he has been a driving force behind the scenes, pulling the detailed content for each title together in the background – working with an equal measure of enthusiasm and patience!

→ **Mollie Dickenson**. Mollie has a background in publishing and works as a research manager at Henley Business School, and has been a supporter of the project from its inception. She has provided constant encouragement and challenge, and is, as always, an absolute delight to work with.

→ **Critical readers**. As the Fast Track series evolved, it was vital that we received constant challenge and input from other experts and from critical readers.

→ **Professor David Birchall**. David has worked to identify and source Expert Voice contributions from international academic and business experts in each Fast Track title. David is co-author of the Fast Track *Innovation* book and a leading academic author in his own right, and has spent much of the last 20 years heading up the research programme at Henley Business School – one of the world's top ten business schools.

The expert team

Last but not least, I am grateful for the contributions made by experts from around the world in each of the Fast Track titles.

EXPERT	TOPIC	BUSINESS SCHOOL/ COMPANY
Professor Bill Donaldson	The changing nature of sales (p. 16)	Aberdeen Business School, The Robert Gordon University
Charles Newby	The secrets of the success of hyper-effective sales teams (p. 27)	Mercuri UK
Dr Robert W. Davies	Sales management – is your strategy good enough? (p. 73)	Cass Business School, City University, London
Geoff King	Using emotion in selling (p. 92)	Author, *The Secrets of Selling*
Professor John Roberts	Sales management in the ascendency (p. 111)	Australian School of Business, University of New South Wales
Professor David Birchall and Jeni Giambona	Getting close to customers (p. 140)	Henley Business School, University of Reading
Cigdem Gogus	Mobile sales promotions – the use of text competitions (p. 160)	Henley Business School, University of Reading
Beth Rogers	Twenty-first century sales management – analytical, professional, strategic (p. 176)	Portsmouth Business School, University of Portsmouth

SALES FAST TRACK

This book will help anyone who wants to advance their sales career. It gives practical advice on how to lead and manage a sales team and reminds you of best practice in all aspects of sales.

As a sales leader it is worth reflecting on what a diverse range of skills a salesperson needs. They need business skills or they'll make few or poor sales, and negotiating skills for the same reason. Then there are their life skills: good communication, huge amounts of confidence and feeling empathy with anyone they meet as they pursue sales. We'll identify all these skills in the book, then show you how to develop them. Compare this diversity with other professionals that we respect, say accountants: they look pretty narrowly at the task in hand and supply the figures that others use to make decisions and run their parts of the company. Not until they're pretty senior does a top accountant need the same diversity of skills that the average successful salesperson needs right from the off.

A salesperson, particularly one engaged in business-to-business selling, has to build rapport with the decision makers, then really get to understand all the customer's needs and wants, design a tailored solution and explain exactly what benefits that particular customer will derive from the solution. And all that has to be done before they start the process of negotiating and closing the sale. Each stage has to move the customer one step closer to buying; it can be thought of as a journey the salesperson is taking the customer through until they buy. A sales leader has to be aware of all stages of the sales process, the tools that can assist, each team member's strengths and weaknesses, and what motivates them to work on the right prospects and customers at the right time. As Greg, the managing director of a financial services company, said to me, 'I have grown up selling and think I'm pretty good; however, now I want everyone in my company to be a better salesperson than me and I will do what ever I can to develop them to achieve that'.

Where does the art of selling start? Well, you have to be aware of the way other people think and feel. You have to put yourself into someone else's shoes and really see things from their point of view. You're dealing with the emotional and subjective aspects of the people you encounter, whereas many other professions are dealing more with hard facts and objective views.

If you go to an optician, the topic is your eyes. Good opticians, though, will ask open questions far away from the subject of eyes, showing interest in something much deeper than your main reason for being there and also getting a far better understanding of how you use your eyes and what strains they may have been exposed to. By getting a better understanding of you and your lifestyle, the optician is not just building rapport, but is also identifying your real requirements and possible future risks; in this case it could be diabetes. This behaviour tends to bring you back to the same optician; they are actually getting a far better understanding of 'you' and are, of course, being a salesperson.

Thirty years ago it was different: people sold products not solutions. In some contexts this still applies; there are still shop assistants who will guide prospects towards the product they want to sell, whatever the needs of the customer. There are still financial advisers out there who will sell the finance product that makes them the most commission. How do such advisers get away with it? They get away with it because ordinary mortals are blinded by their financial science and, in any case, are unaware that it's the wrong product until some time later, perhaps when they have no further contact with the person who sold it to them. The attitude of such a sales assistant or financial adviser offers only short-term benefits. People stop going to a supplier if they feel dissatisfied or ripped off – if, and this is a big if, they have a benchmark to make comparisons against. If an industry is all rogues we'll never know how to compare one product or service with another because we don't have a benchmark.

Benchmarking is an important part of buying where there are criteria other than price, in what we call solution selling. If a buying decision is only based on price, it's an easy benchmark, but this is rarely the case. Where price is only part of the mix you have to try to put a tangible measure against something that is intangible, like service, reliability, fit for purpose, facilitating change, aiding innovation, creating efficiencies, 'making me look good' and your mutually beneficial relationship with the supplier. Sales become more complex when there is no easy benchmark: it makes the buying more difficult and offers the opportunities for the abuse we see so often in the finance industry.

Most large companies don't think much of the salespeople who come to them. Their main complaint is that they take too short a time to understand their business, their strategy and their problems. Here's a quote from a CEO: 'I would buy from any salesperson who asked if they could sit in my office for a week; but do you know, none of them have ever offered.' The impression that a lot businesspeople have of salespeople is that they know a lot about their products and that's all they want to talk about. They're not keen to discuss what their customers need and want.

Ironically, if you talked to the same CEO about his sales force it is very likely that they are equally badly regarded by their customers: this is mainly because of the metrics that they hand down. Often the key performance indicators are based on short-term results and are not designed to allow a salesperson to spend a week researching the needs of one person in one company, no matter what the long-term potential.

That's our opportunity; the Fast Track manager is tasked with leading a team of solution sellers. They have to be aware that selling is a tough job, requiring a wide range of skills and being under huge pressure to meet targets. Just how tough a job is it? Think of this scenario in typical business-to-business sales: when you are cold-calling key people, you will typically get to speak to one in ten. Of those you speak to, you'll get an appointment with one in three, and of those you'll get a second appointment with half. Of those that remain, you'll make a sale to one in three. So to make one sale from cold-calling new prospects, you have to make contact with no less than 180 people. But as you may well know already, when you do make that sale you feel terrific and all the effort becomes worth it. So it's a tough job but also a great job.

For business to exist, someone has to make a sale. Indeed, nothing happens anywhere in business until someone sells something to someone else. There are also very few highs as incredible as when a prospect you have been working on for 18 months finally says 'yes' and instantly half of your annual target is reached.

Many of us move on from this type of selling into getting repeat sales from existing customers, creating a business partnership where both parties are working together to come up with the best solution. This applies equally in business-to-business and business-to-consumer sales. If you have a sales team that focuses entirely on developing more business from existing customers, it is worth considering targeting them on an element of new business selling, as it can keep their selling skills sharper.

From this partnership selling you can move again, this time into complex sales. Suddenly from being the successful lone salesperson driving thousands of miles a year with your briefcase and samples, you're in a team and the buyer has got a team as well. So now you have to add to your skills: managing a team, managing information and managing multiple complex relationships with the target company, perhaps on a national or international basis. You're facing the customer's internal silos and politics as well as their business needs.

Even if you are a brilliant salesperson, don't expect to drop into a new team without having to change some of the ways that you work. You're going to deal with more processes and produce more internal paperwork. On the other hand, don't get sucked into believing that ticking all the boxes in the 'Key Account Development Plan' will automatically maximise the profit from the account. You mustn't lose the relationship-creating rapport or risk-taking part of the task that made you successful in the old job.

In career terms it can be a huge leap to go from a sales role to a management role, and many people find that becoming involved in some team selling can be a good first step in making the transition. It's a time when you're responsible for making the sale but not dealing with the pay and rations of the team you're working with.

From first-line sales management the sky is the limit; you're on your way to being sales director of a multi-million or multi-billion (let's not aim too low) annual target. It's a terrific career and if you want it enough, you'll get there. And if you want it, you should want it fast, so let's get on the fast track.

HOW TO USE THIS BOOK

Fast Track books present a collection of the latest tools, techniques and advice to help build your team and your career. Use this table to plan your route through the book.

PART	OVERVIEW
About the author	A brief overview of the author, his background and his contact details
A **Awareness**	*This first part gives you an opportunity to gain a quick overview of sales and to reflect on your current effectiveness*
1 *Sales in a nutshell*	A brief overview of sales and a series of frequently asked questions to bring you up to speed quickly
2 *Sales audit*	Simple checklists to help identify strengths and weaknesses in your team and your capabilities
B **Business Fast Track**	*Part B provides tools and techniques that may form part of the sales framework for you and your team*
3 *Fast Track top ten*	Ten tools and techniques used to help you implement a sustainable approach to sales and sales management based on the latest best practice
4 *Technologies*	A review of the latest information technologies used to improve effectiveness and efficiency of sales activities
5 *Implementing change*	A detailed checklist to identify gaps and to plan the changes necessary to implement your sales framework
C **Career Fast Track**	*Part C focuses on you, your leadership qualities and what it takes to get to the top*
6 *The first ten weeks*	Recommended activities when starting a new role in sales management, together with a checklist of useful facts to know
7 *Leading the team*	Managing change, building your team and deciding your leadership style
8 *Getting to the top*	Becoming a sales professional, getting promoted and becoming a director – what does it take?
D **Director's toolkit**	*The final part provides more advanced tools and techniques based on industry best practice*
Toolkit	Advanced tools and techniques used by senior managers
Glossary	Glossary of terms

FAST-TRACK-ME.COM

Throughout this book you will be encouraged to make use of the companion site: **www.Fast-Track-Me.com**. This is a custom-designed, highly interactive online resource that addresses the needs of the busy manager by providing access to ideas and methods that will improve individual and team performance quickly. Top features include:

→ **Health Checks**. Self-audit checklists allowing evaluation of you and your team against industry criteria. You will be able to identify areas of concern and plan for their resolution using a personal 'Get-2-Green' action plan.

→ **The Knowledge Cube**. The K-Cube is a two-dimensional matrix presenting Fast Track features from all topics in a consistent and easy-to-use way – providing ideas, tools and techniques in a single place, anytime, anywhere. This is a great way to delve in and out of business topics quickly.

→ **The Online Coach**. The Online Coach is a toolkit of fully interactive business templates in MS Word format that allow Fast-Track-Me.com users to explore specific business methods (strategy, ideas, projects etc.) and learn from concepts, case examples and other resources according to your preferred learning style.

→ **Business Glossary**. The Fast Track Business Glossary provides a comprehensive list of key words associated with each title in the Fast Track series, together with a plain English definition – helping you to cut through business jargon.

The website can also help answer some of the vital questions managers are asking themselves today (see figure overleaf).

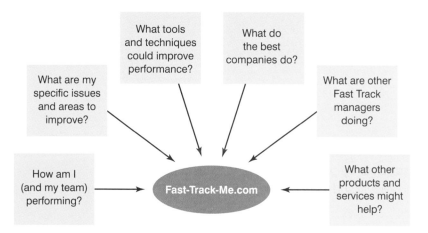

Don't get left behind: log on to **www.Fast-Track-Me.com** now to get your career on the fast track.

PART A

AWARENESS

This book introduces a sustainable approach to sales management and selling aimed at keeping you, your team and your organisation at the forefront of sales, thus contributing towards the future of all three. The starting point is to gain a quick understanding of what selling is and what it is not, and to be aware of your own and your team's capabilities in this area right now. For this reason I will ask you a number of questions that will reveal where you and your team need to improve if you are truly to have a culture of professional salesmanship and meet the aims of selling – an exciting set of solutions for your customers and business processes that will put your sales and service to customers amongst the leaders in your industry.

'Know yourself' was the motto above the doorway of the Oracle at Delphi and is a wise thought. It means that you must do an open and honest self-audit as you start on the process of setting up your framework for sales.

The stakes are high. Selling is at the heart of success in this global, competitive marketplace. Your team, therefore, needs to be made up of effective salespeople and you need to be a good leader in sales. Poor leadership and poor team effectiveness will almost certainly lead to failure. An effective team poorly led will sap the team's energy and lead in the long term to failure through their leaving for a better environment or becoming less effective because of lack of motivation. Leading an ineffective team well cannot compensate for the team's lack of competence. So, looking at the figure below, how do you make sure that you and your team are in the top right-hand box – an effective team with an excellent leader? That's what this book is about, and this section shows you how to discover your and your team's starting point.

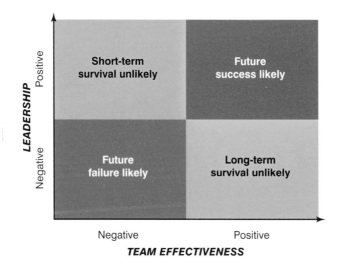

SALES IN A NUTSHELL

This chapter is about awareness of the need for good sales management techniques across an organisation, as well as the recognition that there is usually significant room for improvement in both individual and corporate capabilities and in the effectiveness of their team in achieving results.

Starting with the basics

No business can succeed without effective salespeople. Understanding professional salesmanship is, therefore, a key competency not only for salespeople, but also for anyone whose job has a direct or indirect impact on the organisation's most important asset – its customers. Professional sellers understand the urgency of making an excellent first impression; they know that a feature of their product or service only helps to make a sale if the customer can see how it will benefit them, and they understand each stage of the sales process, from the basics of questioning and listening to leading a customer towards saying, 'Yes please, I'll buy it'. So whether your customer is a consumer in a dress shop or a highly skilled buyer in a multinational, a committee of the board or a middle manager controlling a budget, you need to develop your team's selling skills to make more profitable sales.

Just what is selling?

In many countries, selling still does not have the same status as a number of other professions, such as lawyers, bankers, doctors and teachers. However, the skills required are often far wider and more complex. Sales is no longer just about 'convincing' others that your product or service is better than that of your competitors. It is about taking the customer through a journey where you earn trust and help them identify their requirements – a process they often cannot do on their own – and then provide a solution that improves their own effectiveness. This is, of course, complicated when the customer is not just one person, but a complex collection of decision makers and influencers. The seller can also be organised as a team, with each team member using their specialist knowledge and skills, resulting in careful project management of the sales process. A sale requires a special person with courage and resilience. After all there are few other professions where the people in it fail more often than they succeed.

QUICK TIP *LEARN BY DOING*

If you have a natural aversion to cold calling, plan to do it on a regular basis – try setting aside an hour at the beginning of each day. The more you practise, the better and more confident you will get. It is also worth tracking the number of future appointments you have; come up with a number you should always have in your diary, say 15.

Why is it so important?

Without sales a commercial business has no revenue and therefore no future. No matter what business you are in, you must be selling to existing customers to ensure they continue to buy or that they buy more. It is also essential to continue to grow your customer base by converting suspects to prospects and prospects to customers, and then customers to key or strategic customers: this is the lifeblood of the business.

Effective sales = growth = survival; a business that stands still eventually contracts and dies.

QUICK TIP **SELL INTERNALLY**
It is important for the sales force not to appear remote or
arrogant. Communicate well and often – remember that a
great sale for you or your team often means extra work or
additional problems for someone else. Make sure that
the rest of the organisation realises your vital role in the
business.

So why is it so difficult – what typically goes wrong?

So, it is a truism that selling is important, but poor sales performance is
responsible for more companies getting into trouble than any other
cause. So we understand why selling is crucial, but we also know that it
is far from straightforward to get it right. Consider each of the following
potential barriers and identify which may currently apply to you and your
team, and what you can do about it.

1 **Lead time is extended making the sale later than expected.**
Often called 'hockey stick' forecasting (where the forecast is
flat for a few months and then takes a sudden upward trend),
salespeople and sales managers are frequently guilty of failing
to meet the forecast date for a sale. During the forecasting and
planning process, we estimate as best we can how long it will
take to close a piece of business and the value that will bring to
our company; but there is an awful lot that can have an adverse
impact. Although it is our responsibility to maintain the momentum of a sale, there are many factors out of our control that
extend the lead time. We may find that the decision-making
process is more complicated than we first thought; for example, someone typically decides that they want to get agreement
from a more senior person before they make the decision. The
customer can also change the decision-making process during
the sales campaign. Sometimes the company we are selling to
changes its priorities due to, say, increased raw material costs,
loss of key business or new staff joining. I have seen many
over-optimistic salespeople sure they will close a deal in three

months and it actually takes them 18 months. Or even worse I saw a publishing company involved with a cosmetics company that was going to order a book to go with the marketing material for a new range of products – until the product launch was cancelled and the publisher was left with a lot of time spent earning precisely nothing.

2   **The wrong people represent the selling company.** Every week I meet managing directors who say that hiring good salespeople is their biggest challenge. It is so easy when you have a requirement for two salespeople and you advertise or use an agency once, get 20 applicants, interview seven and hire the two best ones, perhaps the two with the best track record in previous companies. However, just because they were the best of the 20 doesn't mean they are the right ones for you. So many companies end up with the wrong people and only realise it after one or two years. The wrong people are not only ineffective, but they can actually damage your business – damage that often takes years to repair. Not only does the right person need the appropriate selling skills but they also need to fit in quickly with the culture, the people within the organisation and the client base.

3   **The company is trying to sell the wrong product or service.** Companies do develop wrong products and services occasionally, either because they haven't understood the market requirements correctly or because they cut costs in development or production and they end up not being fit for purpose. No matter how good a sales team you have, you cannot sell the wrong product or service. And it can take years to repair your reputation – think of how long it took Jaguar cars in the late 1980s. Once a quality-end manufacturer gets a reputation for producing Friday afternoon products, sales fall off a cliff and take a long time to recover.

4   **Bad leadership from the sales manager.** No matter how good salespeople are, they need support and direction. If this

is ineffective, the sales team is almost certain to be ineffective and may go to the competition. Morale is a very complicated attribute and good sales managers have to maintain it even when results, for whatever reason, are not up to expectation. You can almost smell it when you go into a sales office – one can be buzzing with wit, movement and excitement and another stuck rigidly to screens with little noise and no *joie de vivre*. The happy environments are almost always the most effective in terms of sales.

QUICK TIP **DON'T GO OVER THE TOP**
When times are good it is easy to build morale. Don't let it get out of control and allow your team to become complacent. Remind people how quickly the business world can change and how what is successful now can become unsuccessful.

5 **Lack of support.** Sales can be a very lonely job; salespeople are the 'face' of the company and often work on their own in a store, on the phone or travelling, and being on customer premises. If the support is not there in the form, for example, of good customer service, management-accompanied customer meetings, technical advice and marketing aids, the salesperson becomes isolated, spending their time making excuses or compensating for the lack of support. This takes away from selling time, leading to loss of sales and, in the long term, loss of morale.

6 **Missed delivery dates destroy all the hard work done in the sales campaign.** If the salesperson makes promises regarding delivery of the product or service and these are not lived up to, it is they who lose all credibility, even though what happened was beyond their control. They not only lose that sale but also the trust they had spent months fostering. Word gets round a market very quickly and selling can become virtually impossible. There is then a temptation for the salesperson to

blame the company in order to deflect the criticism away from them. When this happens they are ceasing to 'represent' their company.

7   **There is no agreed sales process in place.** Sales, particularly complex sales, follow a logical process that starts with understanding customer requirements, then discovers the process by which the customer will make a decision, formulates and presents a solution to the customer before handling objections and closing the sale. But a huge number of salespeople present a solution before they really understand what is right for the customer. I have seen this in all sales situations, but it is more common in business-to-consumer selling. We call this 'feature dumping'. It confuses the customer and either means far less is sold than could have been or the sale is completely lost. You've probably been subjected to it yourself, battered by a wealth of information about the details of a product or service that not only does not interest you, but also you cannot understand: yet frankly we all do it from time to time.

8   **No training.** It's funny, we are happy to pay for golf or tennis lessons, but how often have any of us paid out of our own pocket to get sales training? Although golf and tennis are important, they are rarely going to secure our future. We have to be learning constantly, and formal training is often the most effective approach. The trouble is that of all the business skills, selling is the one most based on logical common sense. Everyone thinks they know how to do it but are amazed when they do go on a course to find just how wrong they have been. A key issue for sales managers is a good personal development plan for all their people.

9   **Wrong tools or tools of the wrong quality.** 'A bad workman blames his tools', but there are times when the wrong tools really do affect the way we do our jobs; the right sales tools are just as important as sharp chisels are for a craftsman. The key word is professionalism. Everything about a salesperson needs to be top

quality and professional, from their appearance to their clean car, from the way they get on with receptionists and personal assistants to the brochures and proposals they present – everything. Even a small business has to spend money on the presentation of professional sales aids; any inadequate tool is a major hindrance to making sales.

QUICK TIP **FOCUS ON THE CUSTOMER**

Salespeople will always say where they lack 'collateral' on their products and their own company; yet they rarely seek help with understanding the customer's need. Develop their skills and give them the tools that will help with this.

10 **Not enough sales activity.** It is no use having the right knowledge and skills, the right tools and the right processes if field salespeople do not get out and visit customers and inside sales do not get on the phone. In a normal working week, they should be involved with direct customer work, meetings, correspondence or telephone calls at least 20 per cent of their time. That sounds like an easy percentage to reach, but it is incredible how often it is significantly less than this. An old sales manager I know used to grumble about the cost to his budget for providing coffee for the salespeople: 'Why can't they drink customers' coffee?' he complained, making the need for activity neatly apparent. And, finally, the activity has to be with the right customers and prospects. One danger of having a minimum number of customer meetings for a salesperson to achieve each week is that they will fill up their diary with anyone who will see them. What is the point? Make sure that they are doing the right number of customer meetings, but also that these are with the right type of customer and prospect.

CASE STORY **GOURMET FOOD DELIVERY, REBECCA'S STORY**

Narrator Rebecca runs her own gourmet food delivery company. She had previously developed an impressive network of friends and business associates. After careful research, she created a product that was exactly what a large number of them wanted at their stage of life.

Context Having spotted a gap in the UK market for a daily gourmet food delivery service that offers freshly prepared, convenient meals, Rebecca set up a company working from home. The meals are tailored to help clients reach their health goals, including weight loss. Rebecca thought the idea would work as she wanted to use a service like this herself but found that it did not exist.

Issue Much hard work and intensive research later, Rebecca had 30 loyal clients who were paying up front for ten days of deliveries. Having set herself up at home she already had the necessary equipment to make the business work, i.e. cooker, sink and fridge-freezer. She now needed to move the business out of her home, find premises and buy more serious equipment. She lacked the confidence or desire to ask the bank for a loan.

Solution She decided that her 30 loyal clients were the solution. Rebecca offered them a discount if they agreed to pay for 90 days of deliveries up front. Many of them took her up on this, thereby giving her the finance she needed. It enabled her to set up premises in New Covent Garden Market in order not only to continue the business, but also to grow it.

Learning A good relationship with loyal, satisfied customers can be the source of solutions to business problems well beyond simply making orders. Profit and cash flow are very separate things and sometimes customers can easily help with cash flow if the relationship is right.

So just what is sales management? – frequently asked questions

The following table provides quick answers to some of the most frequently asked questions about sales management. Use this as a way of gaining a quick overview.

FAQ 1 *Are salespeople born or made?*	1 There is no doubt that some people are more natural salespeople than others, and there are common traits of successful salespeople you should be aware of. At the same time, all the skills required to be a successful salesperson can be learnt, and you will be able to help your team members develop the right skills.
FAQ 2 *What are the key traits of successful sales managers?*	2 You will need a combination of coaching ability, leadership skills, knowing when to communicate, the ability to see the big picture and really understanding the individuals in your team.
FAQ 3 *Why do some salespeople stop being successful?*	3 The simple answer is, when they no longer listen and learn. This may mean that they cannot connect with their customers or manage the complex and changing role of a salesperson.
FAQ 4 *Are some sales opportunities better than others or should we go for everything?*	4 Without doubt some are better than others, and these must be identified as early in the sales process as possible. Encourage your team to make a clear Go/No Go decision to avoid dedicating valuable resources to opportunities that will be less profitable in the long term.
FAQ 5 *How can we quickly find out if an opportunity is worth pursuing?*	5 You need to gather as much information as early as possible to help you quantify the value of the opportunity and the probability of winning it. Make sure your team identify all the decision makers and influencers, and look for buying signals. Develop your own simple checklist for this.
FAQ 6 *Is getting the order the only measure of success?*	6 Just because your team members don't get the order immediately, doesn't mean that they have not been successful. Often salespeople go for an order as soon as possible and miss out on a longer and more profitable relationship. Get your team to ask the customer frankly about their sales approach and what they think of them and your company. On the other hand, be aware that some customers are just trying to milk your salespeople for as much advice as possible without giving them the orders they deserve.
FAQ 7 *How do I test if my sales team have strong customer relationships?*	7 Quite simply, the customer is prepared to do work for them. They return their calls promptly; they contact them regularly and ask for their advice. They have cracked it when the two teams, selling and buying, seem almost to be working as one. The chances are at some stage they will be able to use these customers for referrals or references.

***FAQ 8** Why do customers always ask for a cheaper price, however low our quote?*

8 Whilst everyone likes to feel as though they have got a good deal, the reason people ask for a price reduction is normally because they do not yet see the value of your product or service in their language – showing clearly how it will impact their bottom line.

***FAQ 9** Why is it so difficult to get customers to switch from a competitor?*

9 Even though your salespeople may have made a flawless sales approach, they have to be significantly better than the existing supplier, or the existing supplier has to have done something wrong. Only then will the customer accept the effort of switching. And there's a downside risk as well: nobody got fired for staying with the regular supplier but it's more risky if you decide to try someone else. Get your team to ask for a debrief meeting with the customer whenever an important pitch is lost.

***FAQ 10** How do I know if I've hired the right person*

10 Firstly, recognise that you cannot expect results immediately and that there is a delay between what they do and the results they achieve. Then focus on whether they are doing the right things, the impression they are making internally and externally, and whether they fit the team and the company. Finally, of course, there are their sales results.

***FAQ 11** How can I improve the conversion ratios of my team?*

11 There is no simple answer and you will need to look at all aspects of your sales framework. However, you must ensure your team select the right prospects, do the right activities at the right time, maintain the sales momentum, acquire the right level of knowledge and skills, seek the right support and ask for the business. You often get clues by comparing the activities of a successful campaign with an unsuccessful one.

***FAQ 12** How do I improve budgeting?*

12 Most sales budgets are based on past performance with an uplift based on the mood at the time. The only way to budget accurately is to look at your current buying customers and establish what business they will be giving you, and then add to that the likely additional business you will win based on the calibre of your sales team, new products/services and your marketing strategy. The better you know your customers, the more accurate will be your budget.

***FAQ 13** How can I improve the confidence of my team?*

13 Success builds success – the more you sell, the more you will sell. Make sure that you build on early successes and learn from failures, then develop the relevant skills in the team to increase the probability of future success. Don't stint on training and coaching.

FAQ 14 *We keep getting a lot of objections. Can we avoid them?*

14 Probably not. Firstly, recognise that objections are often buying signals – for example, the customer may already be raising issues concerned with aspects of implementation. However, it could also be because your salespeople haven't yet identified their real needs and demonstrated the value of the solution. Take time to regularly improve the questioning techniques of your team.

FAQ 15 *What makes us credible in the eyes of the customer?*

15 Often this comes down to trust, which in turn is a factor of three components: competence (does your team have the skills and knowledge?), integrity (will they act in an honest and ethical way?) and risk (will potential problems be mitigated?) Always do what you say you will do, or if you are going to fail to fulfil a commitment, go back to warn them and explain why.

FAQ 16 *How can I help the team answer the question, 'Why should I buy from you'?*

16 Everyone will be asked this question at some stage, so make sure they are well prepared for it. You can design a template but in the end they have to personalise it so that it comes from the heart and does not sound insincere. Get them to create a number of versions for different customers. If they come up with something that works, encourage them to record it and pass it around!

FAQ 17 *How do we keep control of customer meetings?*

17 Firstly, make sure that all sales calls have a primary objective (what they are aiming to achieve) and a clear agenda. Then ensure they are customer focused and demonstrate excellent communication skills – ask good questions and listen intently to the answers. If the conversation gets off track, check that good questions are used to redirect the answers.

FAQ 18 *Why do sales calls go wrong?*

18 There are a number of potential pitfalls, but the most common issues relate to lack of preparation and poor follow-up. Make sure every call is given the necessary time and attention. A sales call is the salesperson's personal shop window. Encourage your salespeople not to outstay their welcome and not to appear to be working to a script.

FAQ 19 *Why do sales managers keep urging their salespeople to work harder?*

19 Often it is because they are only measuring activity levels (which is easy to measure) and are not looking at what the salespeople are doing or how they are doing it. Take time to get to understand your salespeople and encourage them to ask for your advice up front.

FAQ 20 *Can a good salesperson sell an inappropriate product?*	**20** No, they have to believe in the product or service they are selling and that it will suit the customer. Even in a single transactional sell in a shop, for example, they will be persuading the customer to buy and will lose credibility as a salesperson when the customer realises they have bought the wrong product or service.

I hope that these FAQs give a quick start to getting to grips with being a sales leader. The rest of this book shows you how to move from understanding what the key elements of selling and sales management are to an active implementation of these within your team or division, or company-wide.

The changing nature of sales
Professor Bill Donaldson[1]

EXPERT VOICE

If we are setting a research agenda for personal selling and sales management, the changing role of salespeople must be high on the list of topics. How the sales force is deployed and managed must be a concern for most businesses. Why should this be the case? Firstly, the role of selling is continuing to change and evolve in response to the way buyers and sellers interact. Secondly, personal attributes such as individual knowledge, skills and abilities have been and still are essential, but teamwork and technology are also vital ingredients in an effective organisational response to the needs and demands of customers. Thirdly, the tasks of information and persuasion continue to be performed, but salespeople must take responsibility for creating, developing and maintaining profitable relationships. The implication – a renewed focus on how to win, develop and retain customers to achieve the marketing and sales objectives of the firm.

Sales operations are the revenue-generation engine of the organisation and thus have a direct impact on the success of the firm. What drives this changing role? In part, it is being driven by structural and industry changes. For example, in grocery products 56 per cent of all purchases are sourced through just four buying points,[2] with the result that the size of the sales

---

[1] Further reading on this topic can be found in: Donaldson, Bill (2007), *Sales Management: Principles, Process and Practice*, Basingstoke: Palgrave Macmillan; Donaldson, Bill and O'Toole, Tom (2007), *Strategic Market Relationships: From Strategy to Implementation*, Chichester: John Wiley & Sons.
[2] Mintel (2006), *Food Retailing*, November, London: Mintel Group.

force has reduced dramatically and also changed in the nature of the tasks to be performed. Yet numbers in sales continue to rise. In 2003 there were 766,000 full-time sales professionals within field sales operations, an increase of 9 per cent since 1993.[3] In some industries such as pharmaceuticals and financial services the numbers have risen dramatically. For example, a major European bank employs some 686 business development managers, with many others in managerial and support staff roles across its operations. Hence the need to adopt a different perspective for integrating sales and other forms of communication with the operational side of the business.

Driven by an urgency arising from more complex supply chains, fewer and larger purchase points, the availability and use of IT in customer contact operations, relative increased costs of labour and the continuing internationalisation of business, sales operations are now different. These factors contribute positively to the need for more efficient exchange and communication systems between firms and their customers, predicated by increases in the costs of acquiring new customers and the need to retain the existing customer base and stimulate the purchasing power of those customers already on the books.

Personal selling can be defined as the personal contact with one or more purchasers for the purpose of making a sale. Its importance is such that expenditure on the sales force usually exceeds the budget for all other marketing communications activities added together, with the possible exception of advertising in large, fast-moving consumer goods companies or direct marketing organisations.

Owing to their boundary-spanning role, the sales force of a company has traditionally been a vital link between the firm and its customers and a prime platform for communicating the firm's marketing message and the voice of the customer to the firm. In the high-tech world, it is easy to overlook the importance of personal relationships and how the interaction with customers has changed, if at all. Salespeople have always realised the importance of relationships, but there is now added recognition that salespeople are critical to gaining the maximum value from each customer. Therefore, the management task is to re-engineer sales practices to maximise the value generation potential of the sales force in this new environment.

As a result, the nature of the personal selling task is continuing to change, in that selling to customers has been replaced by cooperating with customers. The goals and objectives for the salesperson have also changed, from achieving or exceeding target, selling X products in Y period and maximising earnings, to building repeat business with the firm's existing

---

[3] Benson Payne Ltd/MSSSB (2006), available at: **www.msssb.org**

and potential customer base. The emphasis has shifted from 'closing' the singular sale to creating the necessary conditions for a relationship between the firm and its customers that breeds successful sales encounters in the long run. This shift renders obsolete many of the currently available sales management practices and the sales philosophy and culture that have driven the development of the sales management field for decades. It also questions sales performance measures based on individual criteria and sales management practices which reflect recruitment, training and rewards based on sales volumes rather than relationship performance. The role of the salesperson seems to have moved away from traditional aggressive and persuasive selling to a new role of 'relationship manager', and, in practice, we are witnessing a tendency to change the sales lexicon from sales force to business development managers, customer account representatives or sales consultants. Perhaps the change in the title is designed to facilitate the transition of the sales force's tasks from selling to advising and counselling, from talking to listening and from pushing to helping.

The new reality of relationship marketing directs salespeople and sales managers to develop long-lasting relationships with their customers based on mutual trust and commitment and shared experiences.

SALES AUDIT

In order to improve performance you first need to understand what your starting point is, what your strengths and weaknesses are and how each will promote or limit what you can achieve. There are two levels of awareness you need to have. The first is to understand what successful sales teams look like and then evaluate how near your team is to matching them. The second is to understand what it takes to lead such a team – do you have the necessary attributes for success?

QUICK TIP DON'T WASTE TIME
The most time a salesperson wastes is working on prospects who do not buy; they often convince themselves that these prospects are right on the verge of buying even though they have been working on them for months or even years. Be objective and weed them out.

Team and self-assessment

Is my team maximising its potential?

Use the following checklist to assess the current state of your team, considering each element in turn. Use a simple Red-Amber-Green evaluation, where Red reflects areas where you disagree strongly with the statement and suggests there are significant issues requiring immediate attention,

Amber suggests areas of concern and risk, and Green suggests everything is good and there is little need for your intervention.

ID	CATEGORY	EVALUATION CRITERIA	STATUS
Sales			RAG
S1	Salesperson – right people	You have an objective selection process and an effective induction process and you keep the right people by measuring their activity, knowledge and skills	☐
S2	Sales pipeline	You judge customers on lifetime potential value; you have common criteria for assessing prospects at different stages of the sales process and you measure conversion ratios at each stage	☐
S3	Market trends	You have a process to monitor external trends: changing market conditions, customer expectations and major competitor activities; you conduct regular SWOT analyses	
S4	Sales planning	You have an effective forecasting process; you allocate resources to the best opportunities and there is an effective forward planning process	☐
S5	Momentum	Customer interest is maintained between visits, and handovers between sales and support people are managed effectively. When the sales process has stalled, clear actions are identified and assigned to rekindle the prospect or qualify it out	☐
S6	Sales process	There is a clearly defined process based on a common set of tools and you have defined the skills and knowledge required for each part of the sales process	☐
S7	Key account management	Key accounts are clearly defined, and are managed differently, and all customer-facing staff are aware of who they are and how they should be treated	
S8	Salesperson – right skills	You regularly review the skills and knowledge of the sales team, then build capabilities through coaching and training, and ensure each member is motivated to learn	☐
S9	Customer focused	All staff are empowered to make good decisions when faced with a customer issue. Your company interactions with customers are based on the longer-term value of each customer. There is an effective customer relationshipmanagement process in place.	☐
S10	Salesperson – right results	You know where your future results are coming from and what will impact them, and you have the right mix of customers in each segment	☐

> ### QUICK TIP *LEAVE NOTHING TO CHANCE*
> Never rely on making your budget from something turning up that you were not expecting. Success only comes from having developed customers through all stages of the sales process.

Do I have what it takes? Sales leadership effectiveness

This section presents a self-assessment checklist of the factors that make a successful Fast Track leader in sales. These reflect the knowledge, competencies, attitudes and behaviours required to get to the top, irrespective of your current level of seniority. Take control of your career, behave professionally and reflect on your personal vision for the next five years. This creates a framework for action throughout the rest of the book.

Use the checklist overleaf to identify where you personally need to gain knowledge or skills. Fill it in honestly and then get someone who knows you well, your boss or a key member of your team, to go over it with you. Be willing to change your assessment if people give you insights into yourself that you had not taken into account.

Use the following scoring process:

0 A totally new area of knowledge or skills

1 You are aware of the area but have low knowledge and/or lack skills

2 An area where you are reasonably competent and working on improvement

3 An area where you have a satisfactory level of knowledge and skills

4 An area where you are consistently well above average

5 You are recognised as a key figure in this area of knowledge and skills throughout the business

Reflect on the lowest scores and identify those areas that are critical to success. Flag these as status Red, requiring immediate attention. Then identify those areas that you are concerned about and flag them as status Amber, implying areas of development that need to be monitored closely.

ID	CATEGORY	EVALUATION CRITERIA	SCORE	STATUS
Knowledge			0–5	RAG
K1	Industry and markets	Knowledge of your industry in terms of scope (boundaries), overall size and growth, and major trends. This should include an understanding of market segments	☐	☐
K2	Customers	Information about major customers, in terms of who they are, their long-term value to you, their decision-making process and requirements at individual and company level	☐	☐
K3	Competitors	An understanding of who the major competitors are, what they do and their strengths and weaknesses	☐	☐
K4	Products and services	An understanding of current products and services and how they perform in the market against the industry leaders. This should include substitutes or solutions available from companies in different industries	☐	☐
Competencies				
C1	Motivating the team	Ability to understand your individual team members: what makes them do what they do and stops them doing what they don't do	☐	☐
C2	Communication with the team	Ability to question, listen, pick up on body language and find the right level to communicate at for each individual	☐	☐
C3	Coaching the team	You set your people up for success, help them achieve it themselves and allow them to analyse what they do well and where they need to improve	☐	☐
C4	Supporting the team	You build confidence in your team to enable them to come to you when they need assistance, development or direction, and you protect them from company politics	☐	☐
Attitudes				
A1	Positive	Belief that you can make a difference and get things done. You are able to face resistance and believe you can achieve – you think, 'I can'	☐	☐
A2	Creative	You are always open to ideas at all stages of the sales process, never accepting that the current way is the only way. You are innovative when matching your solution to individual customers' requirements	☐	☐

ID	CATEGORY	EVALUATION CRITERIA	SCORE	STATUS
	Attitudes (contd)		0–5	RAG
A3	Courageous	You understand risks, are able to manage them and when necessary are prepared to be a risk taker who stands up for what you believe in		
A4	Tenacious	You are prepared to continue to go beyond the 'call of duty' even when the going is tough		
	Behaviours			
B1	Professional	Completing all tasks to a high standard, you come across as a trusted adviser to prospects and customers		
B2	Personal	Ability to relate to others without losing your own personality; you avoid trying to be 'all things to all men', while remaining flexible in your approach to different people. You get the balance right between a flexible approach based on the personality of the individual you are dealing with, without compromising your values and beliefs		
B3	Focused	You can plan, keep to the plan and delegate effectively		
B4	Resilient	You are able to bounce back from knock-downs and rejections as if nothing had happened		

QUICK TIP KEEP CHECKING

It's easy to learn something about the competition and use it in sales planning for too long. They are making progress too.

CASE STORY TOP VEGETARIAN RESTAURANT, AMANDA'S STORY

Narrator Amanda runs her own vegetarian restaurant. She is passionate about every aspect of food preparation, the chemistry through to the emotions, and admits that the success of her restaurant is down to sales, even though she really doesn't understand sales.

Context The restaurant had been voted the UK's top vegetarian restaurant by the readers of a national newspaper.

Issue The service staff were taking orders but did not understand what would improve the customers' experience and encourage them to return to the restaurant more frequently. Amanda had told them to encourage the customers to order wine and bottled water, which they did, but that was it.

Solution The first part was to understand what was stopping the staff from selling. Amanda observed her staff on the job and then interviewed them. It was found that they were trying to turn the tables round as quickly as possible, which in fact was not as profitable as getting customers to buy more and return more frequently. They also were not asking the right questions; so they were given help in developing this skill and Amanda rewarded each of them in a way that suited their individual interests and circumstances.

Learning Get to understand why your salespeople don't adopt best practice, involve them in the company strategy, give them the right training, then understand what motivates each of them – it may not be the same for everyone. Every job, no matter how straightforward it seems, benefits from training.

Learning

Take a few minutes to reflect on the leadership and team effectiveness audits and consider your current position – where are you and what are the implications? How much work do you have to do to get yourself and the wider sales team to the position you want to be in – and, at the same time, can you still deliver the needs of sales campaigns currently under-way? Take every opportunity to develop yourself and your team whilst delivering profitable revenues for your business. There is no better way than learning 'on the job'.

QUICK TIP PRACTISE AND BECOME PERFECT
Always try a new pitch or technique on less important prospects and customers before you tackle the key ones. Also consider conducting role plays with colleagues; it is better to practise manoeuvres in the flight simulator before climbing into the aircraft!

If you are unsure of the need to develop yourself, the sales team or the organisation's approach to sales, have a look at the figure below and assess your current position.

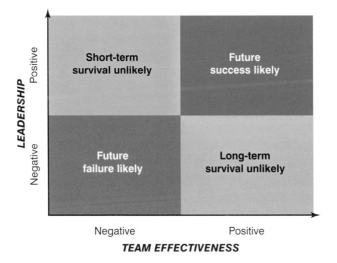

→ **Bottom left – poor leadership and an ineffective team.** This will result in failure. You may already be too late! Take a few key elements from this book and start to make team and individual progress – quickly.

→ **Top left – great leadership but a poor team.** You have a great vision but will be unlikely to implement, it and so it will have little impact. You will need to find a way of taking people with you and introducing systems and processes to improve team effectiveness. How are your communication skills? Have you taken the opportunity to develop people as your sales campaigns progress? Do you have the right people in place?

→ **Bottom right – poor leadership but a great team.** You are highly effective and efficient as a team but may well be going in the wrong direction. It may be that the business is doing well despite your skills, not because of them. Could they do even better if your skills improved? Things are just about all right as long as no major issues occur, but if things go wrong that is when effective leaders are required.

→ **Top right – clear leadership and direction combined with an efficient and effective team.** This is where we want to be. Sales campaigns are well managed and you are taking the opportunity to develop yourself and your team on an ongoing basis. You probably don't need this book, so please give it to someone else!

STOP – THINK – ACT

After reading this chapter you should take a moment to reflect on the results. You will have gained a more thorough understanding of the components that create a good result. Reflect on the profiles of the team and yourself that you have produced. Look for areas where you could get a 'quick win' and improve matters in the short term. If specific areas of concern have come up, then read on – have a look at the contents page and find the chapter most relevant to you. Dip into this book as and when you need it – think of it as part 'self-help guide', part manual, part reference book.

Ask yourself and the team these questions:

What should we do?	What will we change today and what difference will it make (why)?
Who do we need to involve?	Who else needs to be involved and why?
What resources will we require?	What information, facilities, materials, equipment or budget will be required?
What is the timing?	When will this change be implemented – is there a deadline?

Visit www.Fast-Track-Me.com to use the Fast Track online planning tool.

The secrets of the success of hyper-effective sales teams

Charles Newby

The best sales teams manage to achieve great results and they are able to do it consistently. Here are some of the secrets of success; by examining what makes sales teams successful, these secrets can be replicated in your business.

Firstly, hyper-effective sales teams focus on applying the correct quantity, direction and quality of customer-facing activity right across the customer portfolio. This means that effort is applied to retaining and developing existing customers, ensuring that these relationships are as valuable as possible. However, without new blood the customer portfolio can quickly lose its value. Hence the most successful teams will also prioritise activity to build a healthy pipeline of new business. Furthermore, whilst other teams are basking in their success, the hyper-effective are developing brand new opportunities to sell. This may mean targeting new markets, new segments, new territories or just brand new clients, but it is a key to future success.

Secondly, it is incorrect to suggest that the best sales teams do not lose business like the rest of us, and of course a failed bid analysis can ensure that the appropriate lessons are learned. However, when was the last time that you conducted a 'successful bid analysis'? When a new piece of business is won or a major new client is secured there are many valuable lessons to be learned, especially if you can include the client in discussions. Find out what it was that you did better than your competitors and repeat it!

So how do the really effective win these major clients? Decision-making processes are becoming more complicated with the advent of more sophisticated purchasing tactics and policies; however, it would be a mistake to believe that interpersonal relationships are no longer important. Successful sales teams invest time in developing relationships at all levels within their target client. This time is not wasted merely drinking coffee and chatting but is used to gather sophisticated intelligence from as many sources as is practical. Significant efforts are made to understand both the decision-making process and the people involved. Remember, information creates influence and power.

So activities have been planned, relationships have been built and decision-making processes understood; now is not the time to risk all with a 'standard proposal'. It is imperative that the customer's requirements for your product or service are clearly understood. This will enable your offer to

EXPERT VOICE

be proposed or presented to your customer in a way that demonstrates your understanding. Tailoring your proposal does not mean putting their logo on your standard offer – it means describing accurately the value of the offer to their business. Show how you can meet their requirements, be specific about the benefits of your solution and quantify the value that you can create. Vague claims about cost savings or increased productivity are not the domain of the hyper-effective.

Finally, when examining the most successful sales teams it becomes clear that the difference between the ordinary performance and the extraordinary performance is usually in the way that small details are managed. The difference between success and failure at the highest level is often very small indeed. Ensure that your team apply outstanding attention to detail in everything that they do.

PART B

BUSINESS FAST TRACK

I rrespective of your chosen function or discipline, look around at the successful managers whom you know and admire. We call these people Fast Track managers, people who have the knowledge and skills to perform well and fast track their careers. Notice how they excel at three things:

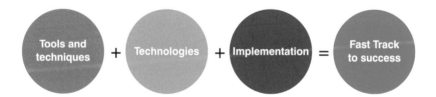

Tools and techniques
They have a good understanding of best practices for their particular field. This is in the form of methods and techniques that translate knowledge into decisions, insights and actions. They understand what the best companies do and have an ability to interpret what is relevant for their own businesses. The processes they use are generally simple to explain and form a logical step-by-step approach to solving a problem or capturing data and insights. They also encourage creativity – Fast Track managers do not follow a process slavishly where they know they are filling in the boxes rather than looking for insights on how to improve performance. This combination of method and creativity produces the optimum solutions.

They are able to interpret the data, giving them a clear understanding of what is important and what is simply noise. They are able to access the right information effectively. The level of detail required varies dramatically from one situation to another – the small entrepreneur will work more on the knowledge they have and in gaining facts from quick conversations with experts, whereas a large corporate may employ teams of analysts and research companies. Frequently when a team is going through any process they uncover the need for further data.

Technologies
Having the facts and understanding best practice, however, will achieve little unless they are built into the systems that people use on a day-to-day basis. Fast Track managers are good at assessing the relevance of

new information technologies and adopting the appropriate ones in order to maximise both effectiveness and efficiency.

Implementation

Finally, having designed the framework that is appropriate to them and their team, Fast Track managers have strong influencing skills and are also great at leading the implementation effort, putting in place the changes necessary to build and sustain the performance of the team.

How tightly or loosely you use the various tools and techniques presented in Part B will vary, and to a certain extent depend on personal style. As you read through the following three chapters, first seek to understand how each could impact you and your team, and then decide what level of change may be appropriate, given your starting point, authority and career aspirations.

FAST TRACK TOP TEN

This chapter presents a framework of methods and techniques to improve performance and make life as a sales team more effective. Each part of the framework can take a lifetime to master, but the Fast Track manager will know which areas to focus on – get those areas right and the team will perform. Often success relates to the introduction of simple tools and techniques to improve effectiveness and efficiency.

Introducing sales tools and techniques

What needs to be included? – the top ten tools and techniques

Selling is to some extent about using your personality to make contact, produce rapport and build trust with a customer. It is also about adhering to a framework of processes that aim to make your relationship with the customer as profitable as possible for both sides. Processes are also to do with efficiency: there is no point in creating close relationships with prospects and customers if it takes the salesperson all year to create them, leaving no time to take actual orders.

So implementing agreed processes with your team is an important element of achieving the maximum profitable sales in the shortest possible time. I see these processes under four headings: salespeople, markets, the sales cycle and customer focus. I explain these briefly below, but will continue to revisit them throughout the book.

Salespeople

People buy from people, not from companies. You can implement the highest quality processes in the land and still fail if the wrong people, with the wrong skills, are achieving the wrong results. No matter how good a salesperson you, the leader, are, you cannot do it all yourself. This leads to the following three key processes.

1 **Getting the right people.** Start off by structuring the right team through a hiring process that includes some objective analysis.

2 **Developing the right skills.** Once you have a good team, keep them producing exceptional results year after year by developing and motivating them in appropriate ways. Agree what skills your salespeople need, what level they are starting from and how you will ensure they develop their skills.

3 **Achieving the right results**. What else do you have to get right to make sure the results are exactly what you and your customers want? Take responsibility for managing the team to produce not just straightforward sales results but also the balance that your organisation requires in terms of, for example, product mix, sales revenues and long-term relationships with customers.

Market trends

To understand a customer in a business-to-business sale you have to understand the market they are operating in, and in a business-to-consumer sale you need to understand what motivates them. The deeper the understanding of the market or motivators you and your team have, the easier it will become to get to know your customers and to propose products and services to help them on their way. I always think it is a good sign if salespeople have on their desks their customers' trade magazines rather than those about the industry they are in. You will almost certainly find one for any industry you are selling to, from *Electronics Weekly* to *Garden Design Journal* and *Investors Chronicle* to *Packaging News*. So make sure you know what is happening in your market or to your consumers, what the key trends are and how to adjust your strategy accordingly.

4 **Identify and use market trends**. Have a process in place to identify opportunities and threats and capture the information so that it can be accessed efficiently. Now use that information in planning your team's activities.

5 **Overall sales planning**. Agree where you want to be, your targets and objectives, and how you are going to get there. This allows you to use a structured approach to setting your budget. Don't forget to document major assumptions as you agree how you will achieve the budget, where the gaps are and how to fill them.

6 **Sales pipeline**. Put a process and measures in place to ensure you are putting effort into the right buying customers and working on the right prospects to enable you to reach your target. Use agreed selection criteria to ensure the team is working on the right prospects and converting them effectively to become regular repeat purchasers.

 CASE STORY ***RECRUITING COMPANY, RICH'S STORY***

Narrator Rich works for a large recruiting company. He has led companies in a number of industries in the US, giving him the ability to place the right employees in each of those industries by having a thorough understanding of their requirements.

Context The recruiting company specialises in filling technical and sales posts. The salespeople they place tend to be pretty experienced.

Issue Sales managers were producing job profiles that were so detailed that it was virtually impossible for the recruiting company to find a candidate that fitted all the specified criteria.

Solution Sales managers had to work with recruiters and human resources to make it very clear what person they wanted and to prioritise the criteria. Rich suggested starting with ensuring a cultural fit with the company. After that they needed to be clear what type of salesperson they wanted, a key account manager, a prospector and so on, and then find out how quickly they understood the 'landscape', knowing where the opportunities are, who will be the right people to network with and so on. Finally they had to look for experience of the industry.

Learning Don't create a specialist profile based on your existing top performers – that is impossible to find. Be clear what your priorities are to enable you to find someone with the ability to fit in and learn to fulfil the role effectively.

Planning the sales cycle

In order to monitor your people's progress in a sale you need a common language to communicate how things are going. If you make this common to all the team, not only do you increase the efficiency of the selling effort but you also allow them to learn from each other by discussing how they took a sale from a certain part of the process to the next.

7 **Sales process**. Draw a map for everyone to follow, from suspect to regular buying customer. Use Post-its on a flip chart; get the salespeople to help. Try it out and adjust where necessary. Make sure everyone agrees to work to the formalised process by making it easy to follow. It has to be to their advantage to stick to the process.

8 **Momentum**. Getting things started is often difficult, but once you have built up momentum it is important not to relax – keep putting in the effort as this is exactly the way sales works. You must keep control of the sales process at all times, moving it forward through each stage in the sales cycle. Ensure that you are getting closer to the deal by continuously agreeing the next steps with the prospect.

Customer focus

Whilst it is important to focus on all your customers, it is essential that you focus on the right customers.

9 **Key account management.** Treat important customers differently. Put a key account management programme in place only if you know what you expect to achieve in addition to your normal sales and profit. Manage and measure the results of the key account approach.

10 **Customer focus.** Make sure you go way beyond the pretty mission statement – 'the customer is king'. Make every interaction with prospects and customers a positive experience by embedding customer focus into the culture of your organisation from top to bottom and by rewarding people when they get it right.

1 SALESPEOPLE *Getting the right people*

How many times have you heard 'sales is all about people; customers don't buy from companies they buy from people'? Quite right too – if you don't have the right people in your team you have a major problem. So you need to ensure you recruit the right people, then develop and motivate them to continuously improve their results.

When you are hiring new staff, consider the attributes they require. If we're not careful we tend to hire people like ourselves, thus missing out on people who will succeed in a different way from us. So you need to be able to measure people objectively as well as by your subjective reaction. I once hired a sales guy who was one of the most unconventional characters you could meet. My instinct was to dismiss him as a candidate after the first interview, and everyone else who interviewed him felt the same way. However, when I scored him objectively against the criteria of what makes a successful salesperson he came out exceptionally high. I hired him and he was one of the most successful salespeople in the company within two years. A word of warning though: you also need to make a judgement call on how they will fit into the culture; you don't want a superstar who just doesn't fit in, gets disillusioned, leaves and upsets the team members in the process.

So, what makes a successful salesperson? They need to have the following attriubutes:

1 A high level of energy to generate a large quantity of activity. I once had a boss who said he wouldn't hire high-energy staff, because all staff are going to 'screw up' and high-energy ones just screw up more often. It was an awful team to work in and achieved very little. I hope no one reading this book feels the same way. In my view salespeople need to be reined back, not pushed.

2 **The ability to focus their effort on high-value, high-return activities**. Any fool can be busy; you need people prepared to stretch themselves and not take the 'path of least resistance', so they need to possess strong time-management skills.

3 **The right knowledge**. Ask your salespeople what knowledge they think they need. You will be surprised at how long this list becomes. They will tend to focus on knowledge of:

→ their company, its processes and systems, its strategy, its culture and so on;

→ the products and services – what is unique and differentiates them from the competitors, what the features are and what benefits these features will give to the customers.

Whilst accepting that salespeople feel vulnerable without good product and company knowledge, you want to move their thirst for knowledge towards:

→ the customers – who they are, what drives them and what their main buying criteria are;

→ the market – what the trends are, where the opportunities are, what the influences are, who the competitors are and what their strengths and weaknesses are.

4 **The right skills**. I'll deal with this in the next section.

5 **Motivation.** This is key. Exceptional sellers need a good deal of self-motivation, but it is still the leader's responsibility to understand what motivates each team member – remember, it is never just money. You need to really understand your people and learn how they respond to different approaches. Be careful; if you ask, 'What motivates you?', you will rarely get the whole

truth, so don't rely on finding out that way. Talking to their colleagues and, if you meet them, their partners is a good way of finding out what makes someone tick. It is also worth observing them outside the work environment. For instance, running a teambuilding exercise is not all about people having fun; it is also an opportunity to see your people's behaviour outside the formal working environment. Observe their competitiveness, their leadership skills and their ability to solve problems and manage risk.

6 **The right aptitude**. You could argue that 'being fit for purpose' is an attribute a leader cannot influence. That is partly true, but there are ways of helping someone develop their aptitude, or build on it. People learn in different ways. Some, for example, learn most by being chucked in at the deep end, others by studying academically, reading books and articles. Some people are more creative at different times of the day – are they larks or owls? Think about your people in these terms, as well as examining perhaps their attitude to trying new things. An aptitude as a seller is not, as some people think, having the gift of the gab. You can develop many different types of people into being good salespeople.

7 **Courage**. This may sound flippant, but one of the attributes I have seen that differentiates good salespeople from the average ones is their ability to bounce back, to accept defeat, learn from it and move on. Remember, selling is one of the few professions where, particularly in getting new customers, you fail more often than you succeed.

Sometimes you inherit a sales team. What do you do then? The temptation is to blame your predecessor for all their weaknesses, or, even more extreme, to ease the team out and replace them with your own choices. However, you hope that whoever hired the team used an objective approach. Don't jump to conclusions; don't let prejudices or past experience cloud your view. Judge them all as if they were new hires and measure them in the same objective way. It is good to be aware that existing teams can have significant unwritten knowledge which you often can't afford to lose.

2 SALESPEOPLE Developing the right skills

Each year we expect our sales team to produce more – more revenue, more profit and more new customers. We want them to take on board new products, create more key accounts, penetrate more strategic customers – the list goes on. And how do we ask them to achieve this? Often by simply saying, 'Do more: make more appointments, spend more time on the phone and write more proposals'. This also results in them travelling more and spending more time away from home. Why do we do this? Because it is easy to measure: 'Last year you averaged 12.6 meetings per week; to achieve this year's target, which is 15 per cent higher than last year, you can achieve that by doing – let me see – ah yes, 14.5 calls a week, that's the plan.' Maybe the first time you do this, it is achievable and it will certainly have an impact on your results. However, next year you will expect them to do 16.7 calls, and that trend simply cannot go on.

QUICK TIP BEWARE DEMONSTRATIONS

Look carefully at your demonstration-to-sales ratio. If you are getting more than two demonstrations for each sale you may be demonstrating too early.

So what else can you do? You can suggest they do 13.5 calls per week and also improve the quality of those calls; seek out better prospects, reduce the closing ratios, shorten the time to close the deal. The problem here is, why didn't they do that last year? If nothing has changed then neither will their behaviour or their performance. In fact, they probably need new skills to get a bigger job done. You cannot expect them to recognise the need and develop their skills on their own. Frequently they are not aware of what skills they require and where they need help. That is where you come in. A good start is to ask your salespeople what they think are the skills required to do their job effectively. They will typically come up with the following:

- → time management

- → research

- → cold calling

- → questioning

- → listening

- → proposal writing

- → presenting

- → objection handling

- → negotiating

- → closing.

If you give them time and ask enough people, they will most probably come up with another 10–20 skills, proving what a complex job sales is. The next task is to measure how well their skills are developed in each category. It's hard to make time to do this – you still have three key accounts demanding to see you, your boss is asking for those two reports and you still haven't done your expenses. But think about the benefits. Improving the quality of your salespeople not only improves their perform-ance but also improves job satisfaction and almost certainly customer satisfaction.

Measuring skills can be very difficult. If it appears to be a subjective measurement it will lead to some awkward conversations with your salespeople. At best they will argue with your assessment, at worst it can lead to serious demotivation. So the key is to make it a formal process with an objective element. You could develop a competence framework; one may already exist in the organisation.

Firstly, decide on a manageable number of key skills you are going to measure. Then have the salesperson rank themselves on a scale of 1–10. Rank them yourself independently, based on observations in the office and out in the field. (If you haven't seen them in action, you cannot measure them.) Be open and frank with them. Pulling your punches to make meetings with members of your team less confrontational does no favours for you, the organisation or them.

You are now in a position to meet and discuss the differences in the scores for each skill. It is vital you understand why the difference of opinion is there and negotiate a score for each that you can both agree on. At that point develop an action plan for what development activities the person is going to take part in and when they will carry them out.

Identify a robust mechanism for helping the person to move forward. Fundamentally there are four ways that people develop skills.

→ Self-development – the salesperson takes responsibility for their own improvement.

→ Coaching – the team leader goes out with the salespeople on calls and presentations, acting as an observer and using structured briefing and debriefing sessions.

→ Training – formal in-house or external courses.

→ Promoting best practice – developing a culture where individuals are happy to share what works well for them.

Identifying the skill and level of skill they need, and agreeing what method to use to help them improve are the job of face-to-face meetings. These can include:

→ Appraisals – the annual opportunity for both parties to discuss the person's skills and personal development plans.

→ One-to-one regular meetings to discuss progress.

Self-development

Encourage the team to read relevant articles and books. Give them a forum where they can discuss selling skills and can learn from their colleagues. Give them opportunities to practise, particularly in low-risk situations like role plays. In fact, encourage role play widely. There is no doubt that if a salesperson has practised handling a particular customer's objections in a role play before they go in, they always handle the objections more confidently and effectively than if they have just idly thought about what the customer is likely to say. You may well have to overcome obstacles in order to persuade some salespeople to do this, since many say that they cannot perform properly in a role play in an artificial situation like a classroom or their own office with colleagues. They can only do it in the live situation. Take a deep breath and explain that research and experience says the opposite of that. If that's what they say in a role play, then that is what they will say to the customer.

Work on developing their skills during customer meetings. Have them review what went well and what still needs improvement. After some time they will become more objective and better at commenting on their own performance.

Coaching

Spend time with your salespeople. Coaching is all about letting them develop their own style and perfecting it. I was coaching a team of highly experienced sales leaders, and they said the way they coach their team members is by showing them the way they have been successful and asking them to copy that. How successful is that likely to be? They said that most of the time they could not understand why the salespeople struggled with the concepts, why they were not able to understand the keys to success that the leaders had spotted 10, 15 or 20 years ago.

If you are coaching during a customer meeting, it is vital that you explain what your role will be before the meeting. The best approach is to let the salesperson run the meeting and you blend into the background. You will initially find it very difficult not to get involved, especially when you see it going horribly wrong. Do try very hard not to get involved; as soon as you say something you will then become the focal point and it will be very difficult to pass control back to the salesperson. Occasionally you will have no choice but to get involved – for instance, if you see a big opportunity that may be lost, but this happens rarely, and in most cases the situation is recoverable. Always debrief soon after the meeting. Try to get the salesperson to do most of the talking; get them to say what went well, what needs improvement and how that improvement will be achieved. Try to get them to do the analysis of their performance first – you'll be surprised how well they do this when they have had a bit of practice. When you offer help, make sure you have set aside time to do it, and then don't drop it, do it. These coaching sessions are in addition to formal appraisals and one-to-one meetings. However, that doesn't mean you cannot set or reset objectives after coaching sessions, just make sure they do not contradict other objectives or actions you have set in the formal environment.

Many sales managers use a tick sheet for coaching purposes. This gives consistency and allows the salesperson to see where they continually fall short. There is a sample coaching tick sheet for this purpose on page 189.

Training

Make the training relevant, as there is nothing more demotivating than sending a salesperson on a course that is too high level or that focuses on skills where they already excel.

The following are some of the options available:

→ **Formal training**. This can be residential courses, distance learning or in-house designed by your training department or an external company. Make sure you prepare your people. The most frequent questions and comments I get when salespeople turn up to a training session are, 'Why am I here?' and 'What are you covering?' They are not sure how useful the course is going to be and often maintain that they know how to sell already. They also don't have any objectives. This is a failure of their manager to put the course into context and on an individual basis to get their expectations and objectives right.

→ **Seminars**. These can be an effective way to learn new skills and network, but select them carefully. It is best to find people who have attended them before and get their views. Often they can end up being run by a number of companies just trying to sell their services.

→ **Internal**. Use team meetings for salespeople to present best practice or case studies. Use experienced peers and other departments who have a particular expertise. Encourage open and frank discussion with no recrimination.

Promoting best practice

Have a system for capturing best practice: use team meetings for a salesperson to demonstrate what they have done well. Use your intranet; simple emailing can be effective too. For example, when an important sale is made, the winning team should email the best insights they have got out of running the campaign. One salesperson I know discovered his products had a previously unknown and major benefit to the customer that solved a longstanding problem. In putting in new equipment in a food processing factory the customer discovered that staff morale had improved and that they could measure it by an improvement in staff retention. The salesperson shared that with his colleagues and they were able to build that benefit into future proposals.

Encourage sharing good practice like that, because salespeople with good ideas tend to keep them to themselves. You may want to come up with incentives for salespeople to share good ideas or what has worked well for them. I once attended a customer's sales meeting. One of the salespeople had recently sold a large project involving the supply of metal cutting and fabrication machines. Initially the sales guy was quite embarrassed about being asked to present his approach – odd, when we think of salespeople wanting to be the centre of attention. After a rather awkward start, he got engrossed in his presentation and there were four or five key learning points each of the other salespeople gained from the experience. One used exactly the same approach a week later and closed a significant deal that doubled his sales figures for that quarter.

Appraisals

You should run these formally once or twice a year, following a set format, normally determined by human resources. If there is no appraisal system in place, you need to devise one. It should be standard for everyone and measured objectively. Do not just measure results but also look at what was done to achieve those results. Measure the activities – the number of customer sales meetings, proposals, quotations, samples and trials. Then assess the salesperson's knowledge; this could be done through discussion or a formal test. It is good to focus on areas such as product knowledge, market knowledge, customers, and then on their skills such as planning, researching, building rapport, identifying requirements, report writing, presenting, negotiating, closing and time management. It is normal practice to agree the salesperson's objectives, targets and training requirements for the following year at the appraisal meeting.

One-to-one meetings

Hold these weekly or monthly. Ideally these should be face to face, and they are more effective if the salesperson drives the agenda, not their manager. The idea is to use this time to get the best performance possible out of the salesperson, by having them talk about themselves and where they think they are performing well and where they need guidance. Again, out of these meetings should come clear action plans.

3 SALESPEOPLE *Achieving the right results*

Salespeople are very good at taking credit for good performance; however, they often struggle to identify exactly what it was that produced the results. Their inclination is simply to claim to be good at the job. More modest ones will say that they were in the right place at the right time. However when their results slip they make their excuses:

→ 'Market conditions were against me.'

→ 'A number of my customers have merged or gone out of business.'

→ 'Rates of exchange went the wrong way.'

→ 'Legislation has made my customers uncompetitive.'

→ 'Don't you know there's a credit crunch on?'

So what does produce the right result? Without doubt the economy has a significant impact. This means that the company and the salespeople have to be agile in taking advantage of opportunities and in mitigating or avoiding threats. The next influence on results is your company strategy, in terms of the products and services you offer and at what price. Then there's marketing collateral, the company's approach to PR and advertising and the quality of your website – and that's just a few of the influencing factors.

Now we come to the sales force – the structure of the sales organisation and the number and type of salespeople that are key to getting results. Then there is the balance between inside and outside sales: you may, for example, choose to look for sales exclusively using outside channels. Another alternative is to have 50 per cent outside and 50 per cent inside, with the inside salespeople handling the smaller but bigger margin customers. In the end the structure of your sales force has so many variables – geography, type of customer and so on – that only your experience over time can find the best organisation.

And finally the quality of the salespeople themselves affects enormously whether you or the competition gets the sale. So what should each salesperson be assessing when they have a direct influence over their own results?

Time management

The first is how they decide to spend their time. One of the great things about being in sales is the freedom it brings. Most salespeople are able to decide exactly how they spend their day. This is a tremendous benefit, but there is a danger that they'll spend their time doing what they like rather than what produces the best results. How many times have you had two customers that you could visit: an old friend who gives you a reasonable amount of business and the conversation is very relaxed, or a very prickly customer who has a significant potential but is only giving you a small portion – they normally have a list of problems and you end up with no extra sales, just a list of actions? Who do you decide to visit?

As salespeople we also tend to like the glory. We love being in front of customers using our sales skills but are not so good at doing the pre-meeting preparation, the research, setting the agenda and objectives, and making an assessment of the decision-making process. Furthermore, we often struggle to complete the actions, or fail to delegate and follow up on them effectively. Taking an action, doing it or telling the customer in advance that you need more time is simple and brings results.

QUICK TIP **DO WHAT YOU PROMISED**
Sometimes the simple things get results. Help your team members to understand that if they want to figure in the top quartile, just doing what they promised will probably have a significant impact on achieving this.

Managers need to monitor activity. I once worked with a company that supplies adhesives to the building and construction trade. The topic was who should be able to look at a salesperson's diary. The managers were unanimous in saying that the sales manager should have access to the salesperson's workday diary. Salespeople are being paid to deliver results and a major influencing factor is how they spend their time, so this should be visible and be measured. Remember again that salespeople are very good at manipulation, so if you measure them purely on activity that is just what they will do and quality will go down – so get the balance right. Let them act unilaterally at times to make sure that your activity recording system, whatever it is, is not stifling talent and innovation.

You also need to give a bit of flexibility. Salespeople often work exceedingly long hours. If they are regularly working late, cut them a bit of slack if they want to knock off early one day to go and see their kids play in the school team, just so long as they don't abuse the privilege. Also don't overdo the measurement. I had one boss in New York who used to scrutinise our toll-road receipts (they had the time stamped on) and if the time was too early or too late he would call us in for a talking-to.

Another impact on results is the team's knowledge of the system. The best salespeople know which buttons to press to get their company, and for that matter their customers, to do what is necessary to achieve their objectives.

Motivation

How driven can we be to get out of bed and go and do a tough job where we hear 'no' more than 'yes'? I have interviewed salespeople whose CVs look perfect, but when you get to meet them, whilst they certainly have everything they need on paper, you just know they are not going to fit in. This is because, no matter what you do, you will not be able to get them to develop the motivation to succeed.

Aptitude

Salespeople must be able to learn and adapt to new and challenging situations. It is important to understand what produced the right results but also to measure not just the results, but the elements that produced the results. A sales leader must be aware of the time lag between what salespeople do and the results being seen. Such an analysis will take you closer to knowing how to improve the aptitude of each member of the team.

4 IDENTIFY AND USE MARKET TRENDS

The least influence you have over each part of the sale is what is happening in the market. It is, therefore, important to have the right monitors in place to ensure that you can take advantage of any upcoming opportunity and plan how to exploit it, at the same time as planning to reduce the impact of any threat.

The market information you need is about all your customers, potential customers, suppliers, competitors and alternative suppliers your customers could use.

With regard to market information, you will need to decide how to do the following.

→ **Capture it**. Your salespeople are an obvious source; they are talking to customers on a daily basis and are gathering information even when they are not specifically seeking it. The marketing department should also help; one of their duties is to be checking market activity and predicting trends.

→ **Check it**. You can't rely on everything you are told. Customers often distort the truth to try to get a better deal, or to make you think that the competition is further advanced than they really are. Verify information gathered against other sources of information and investigate discrepancies.

→ **Store it**. Use your CRM system and work with marketing – they should have a system in place. Make sure you need it before you store it; some information may not be worth keeping because, for example, it is not important or it is not verifiable, it doesn't have an impact on your strategy, it is out of date or it is not possible to take preventive action. Once again salespeople generally don't like 'doing the admin', and also they don't like sharing their own knowledge, so they need some incentive to maintain good records. They need to see what is in it for them. Consider this carefully before rolling out a system to capture market information, because if there is little useful data there, after six months the process will die.

→ **Access it**. There is no point in having the greatest source of market data if it takes forever to get a report out to interpret it, or to find the relevant piece of information, so use technology to make life easy.

→ **Use it**. If you have gone to the effort to collect this data, it would be a pity to waste it. Use it as a reference tool, but also build it into your strategy document and use it to develop new or enhanced products and services.

Examine how your customers are changing:

→ Their perception of you – will they see you as market leader, quality driven or a low-price discount operator?

→ The products and services they will demand in the future – will they be looking for completely different products or services, enhanced ones or more basic versions?

→ Their buying criteria – are they looking for innovation, something to enable them to differentiate themselves or cost reduction, for example?

→ Are they growing or shrinking, and what impact will that have on the volume they will buy from you?

→ Which new customers will you want to target in the future and why is that?

→ Are there products or services not yet developed that will satisfy future needs?

QUICK TIP **DON'T MAKE ASSUMPTIONS**
Always check information about customers even if it seems
obviously correct.

It is important to understand your competitors, so work with your marketing department to find out:

→ Who are your competitors' customers?

→ Why do their customers buy from them?

→ How do your competitors' make money?

→ What are their drivers?

→ What strategy are they following?

→ What is unique about their offering?

→ How are they structured?

→ What are their people like and how are they developed?

→ What about their vision, mission, values and culture – are there
any contradictions?

→ What could you do that your competitors are not doing and
what gaps are there in the market?

You will also need to follow up on lost bids and find out why they went to
the competition.

Be careful not to let tracking your competitors become your major
focus. If all you do is track your competitors, you will stifle innovation
and will always be playing 'catch up'.

All this information should guide you in how you set your prices,
where you concentrate your effort in developing new products and services, how you will market your products and services and how you will
continue to differentiate. It will be part of the planning process that deter-
mines how to develop your people, where to grow and where to reduce
your selling effort.

5 OVERALL SALES PLANNING

I have rarely seen targets and budgets put together in a scientific way. Often it goes more like this:

The board gets together for a budget meeting; they bring in large piles of paper and a couple of laptops and pots of coffee. They analyse past results, look at some market trends, consider new product service launches and come up with a growth number like 7.8 per cent. Then they say, 'Well, if we push it, we could achieve 10 per cent. No, that is too round a number, how about we make it 11.5 per cent? No, let's just go for 12 per cent.' Then they only achieve 6 per cent. So next year they get the salespeople to do it instead: the salespeople present a figure that is either far too low, if their bonuses are dependent on it, or far too high, if they are concerned about their job security, and you get numbers like 35 per cent growth or 20 per cent decline.

In fact, of course, the board needs input from all departments to produce targets and budgets. They have to consider where the company needs to be in three and five years' time and how it will get there. They need to understand the company's capabilities and limitations and have thoroughly understood the market trends. Only then can they produce an accurate budget – a budget that can be used to justify future investment. The important point is that it must be forward looking, not based solely on last year's information – sometimes known as 'driving by only using the rear view mirror'.

Once the budget is agreed, the leader needs to set team and individual targets. It is sensible to set these so that the sum of each individual target is higher than the budget, but not so high that they are, or even look, unachievable. If you have influence over bonuses and commission levels, think very carefully about how they are designed. If you do not have the ability to set them, make sure that you can influence them. They will have a significant impact over the way the sales team spend their time. Salespeople are extremely canny when it comes to figuring out what they need to do to maximise their commissions and bonuses.

Leaders have to work with their salespeople to establish how many new customers and what type of customers they need. How many sales meetings will they need to do at what conversion rate? If that analysis tells them they will not make budget, they will have to work out what they need to change to achieve it. Perhaps they need to see more customers, increase the average spend, improve the conversion ratios, sell more new products, change the pricing policy or increase margins. As a leader you then need to establish if you have the right number and quality of salespeople to achieve the budget. You need to act quickly if you are going to replace people, as it may take time for the new salespeople to perform because of the delay between activity and results. If you can't make such changes, you need to talk to your boss about possibly not reaching budget, but be careful in the way you structure this discussion – have all the facts and be sure you have made the right calculations. Senior managers are not unused to complaints that targets have been set too high.

You also need to liaise with marketing as they have a role here; what campaigns will they run to generate interest and how will these mesh with sales?

At the end of this part of the process you will know where your sales are likely to come from and how you are going to put the sales effort in to make budget.

6 SALES PIPELINE

The function of a pipeline is to take something in at one end and deliver it at the other end. In the case of a sales pipeline it is about taking potential customers in at one end and delivering buying customers at the other. It can also be looked at as a funnel, as the number going in at one end is usually much greater than that coming out at the other in the form of sales. The shape and length of the funnel can have a dramatic impact on profitability. The four big variables are the **quality** of what goes in, the **number** going in, the **conversion ratios** at each stage and the **time** to convert potential customers into buyers.

Often the type of customer a company has buying from them happens by accident. I have met many companies whose boast is 'we go after anything'. This means that any lead, no matter its source, is deemed worth the sales time and effort. This can be very wasteful of time and resources. It also makes future development difficult because the company probably ends up with the wrong mix of customers, with some companies, for example, buying products that limit their ability to grow in the future – ultimately leading to a lower profit than if they had been more choosy about who to sell to. Look at the growth potential of your customers – for example, be careful not to focus too much effort selling components to video cassette or fax machine producers.

It is often an idea to start looking at the end of the pipeline, based on what results you want to achieve and what customers you need to achieve those results. Ask yourself:

→ What does our ideal customer mix look like?

→ What sectors will they be in?

→ What opportunities are there to sell to new sectors?

→ What is the balance between key accounts and others (plus other categories you may have)?

→ Does the 80/20 Pareto's rule apply? (Is it true that 80 per cent of our profits from sales come from 20 per cent of our customers and, if so, is that acceptable?)

→ What will be the average spend of the key accounts?

→ What will be the average spend of the others?

→ Why do customers buy from us?

→ What makes them keep buying?

→ How strong are the customer relationships?

Remember, as you go through these questions you are trying to describe the ideal balance of customers that you want to go through the pipeline of sales prospects and come out as buyers at the end. Don't at this stage limit your aspirations or be overly influenced by the situation as it is now.

Here's how to calculate the number of buying customers required to make budget:

Budgeted sales revenue	25,000,000
Last year's actual sales revenue	20,000,000
Difference to make up, assuming 100% retention	5,000,000
Actual buying customer retention rate	85%
Lost revenue from customers who stop buying	3,000,000
Total net sales revenue increase required	8,000,000
Average spend of new buying customers	200,000
By dividing the total net sales increase by the average spend, you can calculate the number of new buying customers required this year as:	40

Here's how to calculate the number of suspects to be pursued to make budget based on expected conversion ratios:

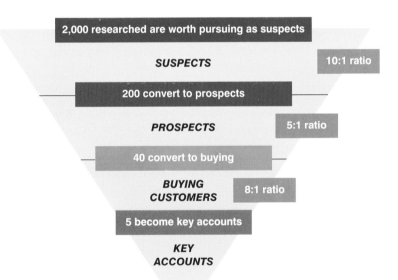

In the example, this company will have to contact 2,000 customers to produce only 40 buying customers.

→ For every 2,000 suspects it has to identify 200 for whom it is worth conducting a sales campaign, giving a ratio of 10 suspects to every prospect worth pursuing.

→ For every 200 campaigns it expects to make 100 proposals.

→ For every 100 proposals it expects to make 40 sales.

→ For each of these 40 buying customers it is able to develop five into key accounts.

Compare the past history of you and your team against this example to create your starting point for pipeline analysis.

By analysing your sales pipeline conversion rates you can adjust your selling activity to improve your effectiveness at each stage. Learn more about the types of prospects who are likely to proceed from being interested to discussing the possibility of buying from you by keeping a record of who you sell to and where you are successful. Change your actions in sales campaigns to make them more effective by using the tactics that give you greatest success. Experiment with the wording of proposals and how you present them and find the way that is most successful. Finally, use the sales pipeline analysis to find out how many prospects you need to make the required number of sales, and discipline yourself to do sufficient prospecting to keep your pipeline full. Most top salespeople have a discipline to spend a certain amount of time each week finding new prospects.

Consider how you generate new prospects – is this from cold calling, from direct marketing campaigns, from advertising, recommendations or word of mouth? Again, calculate the conversion ratio – for example, if you send out 10,000 direct mail shots, how many responses are you predicting to get? What can you do to improve the response rate? You need to establish what criteria the team should use for a prospect to 'qualify' for a sales campaign; communicate this to the team and revise the criteria regularly. If you have to keep 'bending the rules' to get prospects to fit, then it is probably time you reviewed your criteria. An air conditioning supplier firm I know used to have a criterion for its salespeople that they should not chase orders of less than £50,000 or more than £200,000. As they grew in confidence and experience, they slowly increased both those numbers.

You will also want to consider how many meetings you need on average with a prospect to get them to buy from you. What can you do to improve the conversion ratio and reduce the number of meetings to get a prospect to buy? You will need to put measures in place to see how your performance improves over time.

7 SALES PROCESS

How many times have you been in a customer sales meeting and it is just not going right, but you can't put your finger on why? Often it is because you are taking a 'scatter gun' approach and trying to do everything at once, achieving nothing and confusing the prospect. Sales is like any other job or task. You need a clearly defined process: you start with a suspect at one end and you end up with a buying customer at the other end. It is what happens in between that is important. However, few people at all levels – managing directors, sales managers or salespeople – take the time to map the process.

If your company has not mapped a formal selling process, you could experiment with the one below. It is a process that I have introduced to a number of companies and, whilst it may need a bit of adjustment to make it fit your company, it generally offers a quick route into the definition of a sales process:

PLANNING

DISCOVERY

CONFIRMATION

SOLUTION DESIGN

PRESENTATION

OBJECTION HANDLING

NEGOTIATION

CLOSE

Let's take it step by step by looking at the process and using an example from the building industry to make the point. This company cleans up contaminated land in brownfield locations to enable it to be used for housing, shops or parks.

Planning

The more time you spend at the front end of the sales process, the better prepared you will be. This leads to fewer misunderstandings, a less complicated negotiation and a smoother and quicker close. The planning should include the following.

→ **Research on the prospect – what problem or opportunity are they likely to have that your products and services could solve?** For example, you are well aware that in the building industry collecting debt from customers is almost always a problem, so you have a consultancy and training solution to this that could save a lot of money by getting in what customers owe faster.

→ **Contact strategy – who or what functions will you need to meet to build the sale?** You will need to see, amongst others, the financial people who can explain the size of the problem. Maybe that is your starting point.

Discovery

Now you are in a position to plan the first sales meeting, often called the discovery sales call. First of all, set your objectives. At the end of the discovery call you will know:

→ the customer's business drivers;

→ what the customer requirement is, based on the pressing issues they are dealing with;

→ the tactical opportunity the situation gives you.

An understanding of the customer's business drivers makes sure that any proposal you come up with not only solves the customer problem but also fits with the longer-term strategy of the business. For example, perhaps you have found out that, getting debt in is taking progressively longer and that, looking forward, the tight control of cash is a strategic necessity or it will limit how fast they can grow.

QUICK TIP *HIT THE RIGHT SPOT*
Make sure you can start any sales presentation with a statement of a key customer problem.

Confirmation

Now confirm that you have discovered the requirement correctly by meeting with them again, and sending a letter or email setting it out clearly. If you don't do this, you run the risk of trying to solve a different problem from the one the customer actually thinks they have. In the case of the land reclamation company, it has to sell to consultants, architects, land owners and house builders, and this stage is often about getting on to the tender list. Once you have that confirmation you can move on.

Solution design

Design your solution in a way that brings most value to your customer. Remember, the key logical reason the customer will buy is that your solution will bring financial benefits to their organisation. In the case of getting money in quicker, you need to know how they measure their performance in this area. They may talk, for example, about debtor days – the number of days they take from invoice to payment. Your job is to design a solution whose benefits can be expressed in this way.

Presentation

You will probably have two ways to present your proposal, in writing and in the form of a presentation. The key to both is to structure a powerful and convincing presentation that talks almost entirely in their terms.

Make sure the proposal is as powerful as possible by stating who in the prospect's organisation has agreed with your statements. In this case the land reclamation company has to demonstrate how long they will test the land, how they will ensure they get it right the first time and how the process has more reliable results than their competitors. Then they need to describe tangible benefits – money saved, time saved and ability to start building work on a guaranteed day. Whether it comes from the facilities manager or the financial controller: the benefit is much more persuasive if they have stated it rather than you. Assign as many statements as possible in this way – for example, 'The decisions criteria were set down by the consultant'.

The purpose of a written proposal or quotation is to confirm what you think the prospect should buy and to show what the benefits to them will be. It also states the terms and conditions of your offer to sell. It is sensible to rehearse important presentations with your colleagues – get them to give you feedback on the content and come up with some questions the customer may ask. Learn how to present and persuade in a presentation.

Here is a structure for a sales presentation and a written proposal. It has stood the test of time and gives you a shortcut to being persuasive.

1 **Background to the proposal**. This records the activities that you and the customer have carried out to get to this stage. It should display knowledge of the customer and their activities, mentioning the key people you have met.

2 **The customer requirement**. State the customer's requirement with an indication, if possible, of the cost of doing nothing. Try to reflect the urgency of the requirement.

3 **The basis of decision**. This section shows that you understand the criteria the prospect will use to make a decision to go ahead.

4 **Your proposal**. This is a simple statement in the prospect's terms of what you are proposing they buy. Avoid jargon and too much detail.

5 **Vision**. What you think the less tangible 'good outcomes' will look like – the 'wow factor'.

6 **Benefits**. List these as the value the prospect will get from the purchase. Include, if possible, financial benefits as well as other less tangible ones. Where you are claiming that there are business benefits, you should name the person representing the customer who has agreed them.

7 **Implementation plan**. This is a high level statement of dates and key milestones in a complex project, or simple delivery dates if that is all that is required.

8 **Recommended action**. Finally, recommend what action the prospect should take to accept the proposal.

Objection handling

If there are no objections there will probably be no sale. Objections are often a sign that the customer is seriously considering buying. Therefore, there are bound to be issues that they want to bring up that might improve your proposal or reduce the risks of things going wrong. The thing about objections that sometimes we salespeople forget is that we know as well as the customer, if not better, where the difficulties with what we are suggesting lie. So there is no excuse for going into a meeting without being very well prepared to handle the objections. I think role play is a winner here. If you work with your salespeople to practise handling objections, the whole team will get better and better at it.

Don't react to objections too quickly, however. It is a very good technique to try to get the customer to declare all their objections before you start to handle the first one. This gives you a bit of time to think and also to ask more questions that may give you a better understanding of why the customer is expressing these doubts.

Negotiation

The aim of negotiating the final details is for both parties to use some give and take to arrive at a solution that both find satisfactory – the win-win situation.

As usual, preparation is the key. Identify all the issues, major and minor, on which the customer may ask for variations and on which you could make concessions. For each variable, ensure you understand the cost to you and the value to the customer. Decide what your objective is and your bottom line in each of them, and then discuss the issues one by one, keeping strictly to the limits you set in your objective.

Close

Ask for the order, just like that – just ask. Use a closed question so that the customer has to show their intentions clearly. 'Can we move to filling out the order form?' 'Can we go ahead on that basis?' 'Should we get the managing director involved at this stage?' Questions like that make sure that you are still making progress. They may lead to more objections, but they are also leading to the point where the customer says 'yes'.

In summary

During the sales process, people require a number of sales techniques and the skills outlined earlier (on page 40). Think about it logically: if the salesperson doesn't have the skills and knowledge, how can they gain them? If a salesperson is getting out of their depth and needs help faster than they can build the skills themselves, they must get a colleague involved. Maybe someone apart from the salesperson is the best person to negotiate, provide the technical capability, the presentation skills or the understanding of legal aspects of the contract. A sales team should be prepared to help their colleagues where they have particular skills.

There will also be different tools required during different parts of the process. These could be brochures, technical diagrams or scripts to follow. Some managers provide their salespeople with suggestions for introducing a meeting, making a cold call or a quick summary of the benefits of their products – the so-called elevator statement. For example, if you are going to produce checklists of questions and answers to typical objections, make sure you get at least some salespeople involved. Their experience can only add to the strength of the document.

With experience you will find times in the sales process when you need to reach certain milestones. These milestones could include identifying key decision makers, carrying out a trial, doing a product test, holding a demonstration or delivering a proposal.

You can use this experience of these milestones to produce or map your own personalised sales process. The important thing is to produce one and then follow it. Don't make it so detailed that it turns salespeople into robots. I have seen a car company develop a sales process with 39 steps. The salespeople were so concerned with following the steps that they often forgot about the customer sitting in front of them. With some prospects where it is a simple purchase, the process may be very quick. Don't worry about that, just make sure you are not getting it round the wrong way, for instance by coming up with a solution until you are absolutely sure you have all the customer's requirements clearly identified.

8 MOMENTUM

How often have you walked out of a sales meeting punching the air with 'Wow, that went well! They have really bought into our concept and will buy any week now'; then a week goes by and you hear nothing, then two weeks, then three and still nothing? Then you call Mr Blithe and you are told he is in a meeting; you leave your name and number and ask him to call you back. You hear nothing, and then two days later you call again; this time you get his voicemail, you leave another message and another three days go by and you still hear nothing. You call his PA and leave a message with them for Mr Blithe to call you back. Another week goes by and still nothing. When three weeks later you finally get to talk to Mr Blithe, he says,'Oh, we decided to stay with our existing supplier. We liked what you had to offer, but now isn't the right time to make a change.' Why does this happen? The chances are you have done something wrong – you have not created the right desire, not understood their requirements correctly or not understood the value to the customer of your unique offering. Remember that the cost and/or the effort of switching often requires a very compelling argument. Perhaps the customer is simply using you to leverage other suppliers. It is worth investing time to analyse what went wrong. It is very sensible to ask your prospect; they are normally very helpful. Make sure you alter your approach so you don't have the same result in future with other interesting prospects.

Don't hang on to prospects who are not going to order unless there is something specific about your approach that you can fix to recover the lost momentum. Move on and find a better opportunity. This is probably one of the most difficult things for a salesperson to do – walk away from a prospect they have been pursuing for six months or more, especially if the pool of prospects is small. Sure, there is a chance they will buy from you, but there will be plenty of better prospects out there, and if there aren't you need to look at whether you can change your approach.

Always try to leave a prospect meeting or phone call with them wanting more – more information or a proposal, for example. It's a bit like a TV serial; how do they ensure you come back to the next episode? They leave the audience with questions in their minds as to what will happen next. Leave a customer with an unanswered question and the promise that you will return with some valuable information. Maybe at the beginning it's best to give only a partial solution. The temptation is to give them everything you can to help them as much as possible. Try to hold back, even if you have seen exactly the same situation in the past and you know just what needs to be done. Wait until they sign on the dotted line before you give everything away.

Sometimes you just cannot get a prospect to buy despite the fact that they are still willing to see you and seem happy with your proposition. Somehow the momentum has gone out of the sales process. This is dangerous because you risk wasting your time or, if someone else could make more progress, you risk actually losing a sale. In such situations you need to pass customers or prospects on to other people. Maybe an outside channel or agent would be more likely to close the sale. Maybe someone who knows the customer's industry better might be the right person, and moving the prospect from a sales executive to a key account manager is the answer. Or you could need someone more senior like the sales director to remove the log-jam and move the sale on.

When you move the sale to someone else, you need to understand why the prospect has come this far with you already. What is it about you (not the company, product or service) they like? What specific key information or insight do you have that has enabled this relationship to develop, albeit without a commercial conclusion? You will need to understand what these are to maintain continuity when you hand over responsibility. The temptation is to introduce your colleague to a few of the customer's key decision makers and then say, 'Over to you chum'. This rarely works, and ironically shifts the onus and workload to the customer to maintain the relationship. Often they get frustrated or insulted and walk away. The incumbent gets blamed and your company loses a potentially valuable piece of business. Invest the time early in this handover period; don't wait for it to go wrong, it is always worth the effort.

Detect a loss of momentum as early as possible and take action quickly. A sales manager I know had a salesperson with huge enthusiasm and energy who produced a long list of prospects, all of whom seemed to be keen. But the promised stream of steady orders did not materialise. Sensing the lack of momentum, the manager called the prospects and asked the simple question, 'I have to organise our support resources and I wondered if you had thought about roughly when you would require them'. This very low-key closing question revealed those prospects who were keeping the relationship going but actually had little intention of buying. The manager left the ones who answered positively with the salesperson; the ones who did not were either taken off the prospect list or moved to another sales resource.

9 KEY ACCOUNT MANAGEMENT

There are probably as many definitions of the term 'key account' as there are people who use it. So often we promote the biggest spenders to the lofty status of 'key account' without really understanding what's in it for the business and what's in it for the customer. I'm going to try to answer the question, 'How do you manage a key account?' but let's start with what constitutes a key account. Here's an example of how not to do it. I have a colleague at Mercuri who previously worked at a computer component supply company. IBM, one of the largest computer manufacturers and provider of global software, systems and consultancy, was their biggest customer, contributing 30 per cent of their sales turnover. The managing director was horrified when my colleague called a meeting to recommend they get rid of IBM as a customer as they were losing money on the sales they made to them. IBM's position as a key account had attracted such discounts and concessions it had become impossible to make a profit out of them. The MD was shocked and pointed out the gargantuan size of the customer, their contribution to overheads and their history of buying their products from when they started up the company.

This situation can help us to understand the choice of key accounts: who is right? On the one hand, it cannot be right to continue to deal with a customer on a long-term basis if you can't make any money from the relationship. On the other hand, you are dealing with a major player. It's a great source of market and competitive information and a key reference for the salespeople to use with other prospects. It has to be worthwhile negotiating a better deal, and that is what they did.

They didn't drop IBM as a customer, but they worked with them, pointing out the fact that they cost them money. They worked together to re-evaluate products and prices and within a few months the transaction became profitable. There can be examples where you can justify having a large customer where the profit is small or even where they make a loss. For example, status – the fact you do business with the biggest company in the sector – could be important if you get a significant portion of your profitable business from companies who will only do business with you because you work with an important player in their field. There may be economies of scale that bring down your production cost per item. Or there could be associated business where a loss leader is a lever to other profitable sales, either to that customer or sister companies.

As with the sales process your company needs a process for defining the objectives of treating some customers differently from others, selecting the customers who qualify for key accounts, managing the account and planning for the future.

Here is an example of this process you can use as a template:

WHY?	WHICH?	HOW?	BEYOND
Increase or project: • profit • revenue • PR opportunities to generate other business	Selection criteria: • total sales • total profit • strategic importance • future potential • fit with our business	Management: • people • contact strategy • communication • measurement • information • internal processes • review meetings • stability indicators	The future: • alignment of objectives • customisation • influence on our strategy • innovation • long-term mutual growth

Why?

Often companies introduce a key account programme just because that is the thing to do, and there is no thought as to how to align it to their own strategy. At its most basic, it is about the Pareto principle – protect the 80 per cent of results being produced by 20 per cent of sales and support effort. Don't spend 80 per cent of the effort to get the extra 20 per cent. Do be clear why you are doing it and communicate the reason internally (and to some extent externally). The attention of a key account manager and perhaps a team should result in improved profits and revenues, and just as importantly it should make sales more predictable because the relationship includes a certain amount of mutual planning. Indeed some have defined the relationship between a supplier and its key account as, 'The customer is involved in our plans and we are in theirs'.

The exchange is that you are privy to their way ahead, which gives you an edge over your competitors, and in return they have the ability to influence your resourcing, budgeting and even product plans.

There are other 'soft reasons' for treating a customer as a key account in terms of their PR and promotional value.

Which?

Be careful not to select key accounts on emotion, because they were your first customer or because they have become friends. The checklist in the diagram is useful in making sure that you choose the right companies for the right reasons. Remember, one downside of selection is that other customers may get to realise that they have not been selected. Another downside is that the customer gets the view that they are very important to you and negotiates very hard for more discounts and better treatment. Selection on profit, current or future, is probably one of the key criteria. Also be cautious of promoting customers to key accounts because they shout loudest. I have a theory that customers who are on to you daily about the quality of your products or services, your customer service, the information flow and your pricing structure are doing this because they don't have an option, or the cost to them of switching is too great. If they had alternative sources of supply, they would just switch. The silent ones are those you need to worry about.

How?

It is very important to plan account management carefully, and it may have an impact on the way you structure your team. Make sure that everyone knows which customers you are working to develop into key accounts. If you have great salespeople with the potential to move into management, then it is useful to promote them into the role of key account manager in order to develop their management skills – one of the key skills will be how to influence a large team who do not report directly to them – without creating debilitating bureaucracy.

Think through the decision-making process and people in your key accounts. This gives you a chance to develop a contact strategy. Many senior people at your customer may insist, for example, on talking to senior people on your side. This strategy is probably a matrix of who meets whom and how often per year.

Develop a communication plan that makes sure your name is in front of the customer's most important people regularly, perhaps through a newsletter developed jointly between you and your customer. Measurement is essential. A key account can mop up resources and you must make sure that you are getting good return on your investment.

By the time a company has managed a key account for a number of years they should have very detailed information on the customer's business, in some cases this will be as much information as the customer has themselves. Think through how to retain this information and make it available to anyone who gets involved. One very good idea is to have a summary document that describes the customer – its history and its key people, as well as its numbers and what you are trying to achieve. This could be contained in your CRM system, so that it is easy to brief anyone, a senior manager or technician from your side, who has to talk to the customer at some level.

QUICK TIP **DIFFERENTIATE BETWEEN SUPPORT PEOPLE**
Remember that a director needs different customer information from a maintenance engineer.

Have measures in place to ensure your internal processes are being followed correctly and that each stage is producing the right outcomes. If there are issues, it could be because the processes are not the right ones and need to be reviewed.

I recommend that you hold regularly scheduled review meetings with your key accounts. If possible use a standard agenda that can be 'flexed', depending on each key account's requirements. Measure the outputs from these meetings. For instance: actions (what, who and by when); feedback on your processes; perception of you as a supplier; and what they think of your contact strategy.

It is worthwhile introducing objective stability indicators to measure how strong your relationship is and how likely they are to switch away from you. This will give you an idea of how to strengthen your relationship – for instance, you may not have covered all the decision makers effectively, or your complaint handling process may not be working for a particular department.

Beyond

Your overall strategy is to maintain an alignment between what you and the customer are trying to achieve. This means understanding their strategy and key business issues. Use the relationship with your key accounts to drive innovation. The depth and breadth of your relationship will allow you to have candid sessions with them, identifying ways to innovate your product or service, ways to market, how you sell, how you are structured or your processes. Customising a solution is very good indeed for your reputation with that customer, but take the time to calculate the return on investment. It can be a costly business and if you are not going to make money you will have to limit how much you customise your offering.

Make sure that any influence the customer has on your strategy is agreed with others in your organisation. Too often we react to a key account threat or demand, change something and muck up an important internal strategy such as the marketing plan.

The ultimate aim of a key account strategy is to generate long-term mutual growth, where you work jointly to reduce each other's costs, drive efficiencies and improve opportunities to increase sales and margin.

I recently met managers from a large worldwide airline who told me that many of their suppliers are so intent on not losing their business that they are no longer prepared to take risks and are failing to challenge them. As a result they offer few new ideas and little spur to innovation. Make sure you do not allow the key account management process to stifle new ideas and stagnate the relationship and your own development. Capture best practice, ideas and knowledge from key accounts and then develop them as opportunities for growth, such as new processes, new products and services, new markets and new customers.

10 CUSTOMER FOCUS

Nowadays it is probably unusual for a company not to make public statements saying that the customer is at the heart of their organisation or that the customer is king. When you walk into the reception of hundreds of companies, they have big plaques on the wall advertising their customer-focused mission statement. The statements may be the opinion of the board but just promulgating them isn't what produces a customer-centric organisation.

Consider a customer-focused culture in the following two areas.

1 **The actions of senior management**. I have dealt with many companies who say that the customer is at the centre of their business, yet the senior managers never, and I mean never, visit a customer. They devise strategies that talk about satisfying customers' changing demands, but the strategy ends up being 'How can we grow our business/increase our margins/'reduce our costs?'. If you don't know your customers, the strategy is going to be either a very short-term success or pure guesswork.

2 **Staff attitude**. The best example of good staff attitude I have ever experienced is with a phone company – probably the last type of company you would expect to use in a 'how to' rather than a 'how not to' example. I had a problem with a new connection; I called and the person answering took down my details and said that they couldn't help but would pass me to someone else. I was fully expecting to have to repeat everything I had just said, but no, they had passed all this information through already. The new person introduced herself, explained her role and called me by my name all the way through the call. I was very annoyed by the problems with the connection and was ready for a fight. However, she started by showing empathy, then asking a number of very good questions to understand exactly what the problems were. She had the authority to make decisions and made it clear which were the areas where she couldn't make decisions and why. She gave me confidence that she would fix my problem and gave me her direct number in case there were any other problems. She treated my problem seriously, developed mutual trust and acknowledged that it was the company's responsibility. Subsequently she resolved the problem and checked that the situation was resolved to my satisfaction. Not a bad summary of the aim of a customer-focused culture.

How customer focused are you?

So, how can you tell whether you have achieved a customer-focused organisation? What is your starting point? The best way is to ask your customers. You can do this either informally or formally.

1 **Informally**. Good questions to ask customers in a meeting are, 'What do you think of us?' 'How are we performing?' 'How is it when you deal with us?' If you do this, ensure you are capturing the feedback and that it is not being skewed, either in the capture or in the way the questions are phrased. Salespeople are not necessarily the best sources of this information. They are pretty clever at getting customers to say things that bring the sales side out in a good light, possibly at the expense of everyone else.

2 **Formally**. Use customer surveys to establish their perception of you. You can get help from consultants or the internet on how to develop written or online questionnaires and focus groups. We all feel surveyed to death, so ensure that it is in the customer's best interest to respond. The customer has to feel that if they cooperate they may see changes for the better. If you do make changes as a result of such questionnaires, make sure you go back to the people who responded and let them know. Simple checks on a questionnaire are 'Is it relevant?' 'Is it short enough?' and 'Is it easy to complete?'

Depending on your industry you can also try mystery shopping. I have dealt with companies that feel this is underhand, and that if their staff found out they would realise that to some extent their managers are checking up on them. Even if this attitude exists in your company, I suggest you still engage in mystery shopping and work at the same time on changing staff attitudes by showing them the benefits to them, the customer and the organisation of using this method. You may need to do some more work beforehand in positioning it well. The bottom line is that everyone should be proud of doing a good job and would welcome this being recognised. They should also be prepared to identify where it is not going so well and need to improve. Don't design the exercise to catch people out or humiliate them. Try to reward them for getting it right rather than criticise them for getting it wrong. Once you have done the research, do make the changes and communicate them both internally and externally.

Being customer focused does not mean losing a company focus; decisions must be in the best interest of both the customer and your company. Customer focus involves the whole company and its culture.

STOP – THINK – ACT

At the end of this chapter you will have learned about what makes a successful sales team and how to lead them effectively. The chapter has included a variety of tools and techniques used by the world's most successful companies to optimise their sales performance. Some will be more relevant than others and some may need to be adapted to suit your specific situation. Take time now to reflect on the top ten sales tools and techniques, and identify elements that you will include in your sales framework.

What should we do?	What tools and techniques are appropriate?
Who do we need to involve?	Who needs to be involved and why?
What resources will we require?	What information, time, people and budget will be required?
What is the timing?	How long will each activity typically take?

Visit **www.Fast-Track-Me.com** to use the Fast Track online planning tool.

Sales management – is your strategy good enough?

Dr Robert W. Davies

EXPERT VOICE

Every organisation needs a strategy, a route map to achieve its objectives – that is common sense. But how do you know whether or not your organisation's strategy provides a firm foundation for the sales process? Does the strategy, for example, clearly identify who the target clients really are, how you will get to them and, most importantly, the unique features of your organisation's offerings? Or are there areas that have been omitted or are ambiguous?

Without a *complete* strategy the possibilities are that the sales process will falter or fail as you progress down the path of implementation. So, how do you know if your strategy has critical omissions? Here I will develop a checklist of key questions that will help you determine whether or not your organisation's strategy is fit to support the sales process.

Hambrick and Fredrickson[1] provide us with some important pointers on what a strategy should contain – the dimensions to look for when you review your organisation's business plan. They hold that a strategy consists of five dimensions:

→ the arena

→ the differentiators

→ the vehicle

→ the economic logic

→ staging.

We will now look more closely at each of these dimensions.

The *arena* answers the question, 'Which client segment(s) are we targeting?' We must understand who our target clients are, which of their needs we are satisfying, where the target clients are located and what product categories we are focusing on.

Whilst all of the five dimensions are important, and an effective strategy cannot exist without all five, the second dimension, *differentiators*, arguably is of central importance. As its title suggests, the focus is upon how your organisation's offerings, its products and services, are going to be different and display some uniqueness when contrasted against those of your competitors. Ideally, as Anderson, Narus and van Rossum[2] argue, your differentiators should make your offerings resonate with your clients. In other words, your offerings should create value for your clients in some unique way that is of central importance to them. Without clearly defined differentiators that really matter to your clients, there may be nothing left but price to negotiate over as the sales process progresses.

The *vehicle*, the third dimension, explains how the organisation is going to gain the desired presence in its chosen arena. Are we going to concentrate upon our current offerings or are we going to develop totally new offerings? Are we going to concentrate on our existing markets or are we going to break out and serve new markets? Are we going to grow organically, acquire, enter into a joint venture or divest?

[1] Hambrick, D.C. and Fredrickson, J.W. (2001), 'Are you sure you have a strategy?' *Academy of Management Executive*, 15 (4), 48–59.
[2] Anderson, J.C., Narus, J.A., and van Rossum, W. (2006), 'Client value propositions in business markets', *Harvard Business Review*, 84 (3), 90–99.

Economic logic identifies how your organisation will generate the planned financial returns. Broadly, is this through a lower cost operating base or features of your offering that can command premium prices? The mechanism to deliver financial returns must be clearly identified.

As one would expect, the final dimension, *staging*, is concerned with implementation. What moves and sequence of actions do we plan to take to make the strategy come to life? Do we have a clear set of milestones so that we will know where we are in our journey? In short, is there an agreed implementation plan?

But are there other dimensions that we should consider? I would argue that there are two.

Firstly, it is hard to find any market that is not changing. Technology and globalisation are two forces, amongst others, that have and will continue to reshape our world. We therefore need a clear *vision of the future*. The vision of the future presents us with a view of how our arenas or markets will change and the challenges and opportunities that we must face. This vision of the future provides us with an essential foundation for the development of the five dimensions that we have discussed above. The view of the future must be clearly documented and communicated. If new trends occur, we need to be able to identify them and formulate a response before our competitors do.

But there is a seventh and final dimension that must be considered. If your organisation aspires to grow and to achieve more than it has done before, then implementing your strategy will involve change and total commitment. Kotter[3] tells us that the first step towards successful change and transformation is the creation of a sense of urgency. That is exactly what a strategy must be capable of delivering. A sharp, easily communicable message that explains why action is needed *now*. I call this final dimension the *strategic story*.

So in all we must look for seven dimensions. If any one is omitted or is incomplete, failure is on the horizon. The following questions may help you to evaluate your strategy:

✗/✓

1 Do you have a clear, documented view of the shape of the future marketplaces for your offerings (the *vision of the future*)?

2 Are target clients and their needs clearly identified (the *arena*)?

[3] Kotter, J.P. (1995), 'Leading change: why transformation efforts fail', *Harvard Business Review*, 73 (2), 59–67.

3 Can you explain how your organisation will
   create resonating client value (the *differentiators*)? ☐

4 New or improved offerings, new markets, acquisitions
   and joint ventures – have you defined how you are
   going to build your desired market position
   (the *vehicle*)? ☐

5 Can you explain how your offerings and business
   processes will deliver profit (the *economic logic*)? ☐

6 Have you defined how you will build the resources
   and capabilities that your business needs (*staging*)? ☐

7 Does the *strategic story* inspire action and
   commitment? ☐

TECHNOLOGIES

To remain as effective and efficient as possible, Fast Track managers differentiate themselves by the support mechanisms they put in place to help themselves and their team. These include the intelligent use of appropriate technologies – enabling, for example, the automation of non-core activities, thereby freeing up time to focus on the customers and to manage, motivate and lead people. They may also include the use of coaches and peer-to-peer networks, and gaining access to the latest thinking in their field.

Getting started

Everyone agrees that sales is largely about people buying from people; so we might conclude that technology can only have a limited influence on performance. Whilst technology can never take over the relationship side of selling, there are a number of technologies that can assist salespeople and sales managers to reduce the time taken to do less important tasks. Technology should be used as an enabler, without interfering with the essence of what sales is all about.

There are certain implications of the wider use of technology, both internally and in relation to customers.

Internally, the implications are as follows.

→ Everyone has faster and better access to customer and competitor information.

→ It is easier to track trends, opportunities and threats.

→ You can measure your salespeople's activity, knowledge and skills.

→ Technology can be very effective in sharing best practice.

→ It can create more administration and salespeople can use problems with the system or bureaucracy to make excuses for non-performance.

→ It can cause information overload.

I was holding a workshop on internal communication with a client and all attending were complaining that they didn't know what was happening inside the company. When we discussed it further it became apparent that they actually did have all the information that they needed to be effective. Either they weren't looking at it, would glance at it but leave for later analysis (which they never got round to), or had forgotten where to find it. So the issue is not only to ensure that everyone has access to the right information but also that they use it effectively.

In relation to customers, there are the following implications.

→ **In the past one way salespeople added value was to keep the customer informed of new ideas and trends.** Nowadays, customers, who are using technology themselves, are better educated and may well know more than the salesperson as to how a product or service can match their requirements, often making the salesperson feel redundant. Now that the customers can do so much more for themselves, salespeople have to do far more to add value.

→ **Customers can opt for multiple ways to buy, even in business-to-business for instance, using internet auctions or tenders.** The benefits to them of doing this is:
  → avoiding the need for sales visits;
  → widening the range of possible suppliers, for example enabling them to buy direct from China without using a local distributor or agent;

→ making it easier to compare prices, resulting in suppliers com-
moditising their products, offering them with limited after-sales
service.

QUICK TIP **IS IT USER FRIENDLY?**
A poorly presented ordering procedure can lose you more
customers than it gains.

Top technologies

Throughout the sales process, there are a number of technologies that
can help the effectiveness of sales managers and salespeople. There is
a wide range of benefits that technology can bring to sales, many of
which fall into the four areas shown in this model:

Review the following technologies within this context – then decide how
you can embrace technology to improve your team's effectiveness.

1 Scanning customers and competitors using the internet

What is it?

The internet or World Wide Web (www) is a network of interconnected computers. It enables the sharing of information anywhere in the world, so long as you have the necessary access. Information on your customers and competitors is now much more freely and quickly available.

Pros

It can speed up the sales process by enabling you to research prospects before any contact is made, reducing time wasted on poor prospects and reducing the quantity of information you need to gather in face-to-face meetings.

You can gain competitive advantage by using the internet in a more effective way than your competitors. (Consider applying some of the success factors listed below.)

It is free, it gives you instant access and you can gather opinions as well as facts.

Cons

Not all information is accurate or up to date.

Competitors have the same information as you.

Customers can also research you and may deselect you because of information they gather.

It can create 'information overload'.

Success factors

Validate the knowledge gathered against at least one other source. Check the date when it was written and bookmark trusted sources that work for you.

Ensure you do not spend too much time getting sidetracked and gathering knowledge with little use. Setting time limits can be useful, as it is easy for two hours to go by when you only meant to invest 20 minutes.

Consider setting up knowledge/information feeds, where information comes to you without your searching, and then scan for usefulness.

Do not tell your customer how much you have found out about them, but use the information to set relevant objectives and design good questions.

How does it fit?

Sales process: Speed up the sales process by doing more research up front and find hooks or clues that indicate the better prospects.

Customer relationship: Use your company's website to deliver the appropriate experience and image to your customer.

Communication: It provides topics to maintain regular communication with your customers.

Knowledge: Use the web regularly to improve your customer, market and competition knowledge.

2 Business networking

What is it?

Business networking on the internet. This is probably still in its infancy. For people who have grown up using social networking sites, the natural next step when they get into sales is to use business networking sites to build a network to identify future sales opportunities or potential new employees.

Pros

It can create a large and effective network very quickly.

Many companies use business networking sites on the internet to generate sales leads.

It allows you to find people to share ideas with and ask questions or test theories.

You could find very good potential new salespeople, even if they are not looking for a job (sometimes they are the best).

Cons

All the information you and your employees post is open to everyone.

People may link to you who, at some stage, you may prefer not to be associated with.

If you are not careful it can be very time consuming with little tangible payback.

Success factors

Measure the benefits and compare them with the time you spend – is it worth it?

Scrutinise the information you and your team members include on their pages – it could easily send the wrong or mixed signals.

Do quick scans little and often.

Whatever your views, do not ignore this technology, because there will be plenty of your competitors out there who are keen to find an angle to create a competitive advantage using the information these networking sites are so rich in.

How does it fit?

Sales process: It may be possible to shorten the sales process by identifying prospects or the right contacts within a prospect.

Customer relationship: A better knowledge of individual decision makers can allow you to tailor your service and improve the relationship.

Communication: You can communicate quickly, formally or informally with a large number of contacts.

Knowledge: You can improve your knowledge of people – key decision makers, potential new employees, your own employees and your competitors.

CASE STORY *INTERNATIONAL AGRICULTURAL MACHINERY MANUFACTURER, TREVOR'S STORY*

Narrator Trevor is the European sales director for an international agricultural machinery manufacturer. He has been with the company for 15 years.

Context The company decided to implement a CRM system. It also planned to use the opportunity to improve the coordinated management of customers between the sales and marketing departments.

Issue While head office wanted to control and observe global marketing effort, it also wanted to transfer the cost of the new system to each country unit. However, many country managers were resistant to paying because they did not understand the benefits to them of improved market communications.

Solution Trevor delayed the rollout of the system until the right people were trained in how to identify value, create value and demonstrate value to the customer.

Learning People make the technologies work. CRM implementation can be very expensive and only justifiable at a certain return on investment. That payback will not happen if the people are not aligned to the implementation of the technology. A global rollout of professional sales culture and skills development must be the first step.

3 Lessons-learned database

What is it?	A central repository of the lessons learned, populated by members of the sales team. It captures best practice that has worked at all stages of the sales process, including selection criteria, warm-up letters, agendas and power questions (ones that really make the customer think and get high-quality information). Then there are presentations, typical objections and best responses. You can also include negotiation case studies. For instance, a salesperson in a company selling connectors into the car manufacturing industry came up with an email follow-up template that worked so well that she had it designed into the company CRM system.
Pros	You avoid reinventing the wheel and save time. You create a culture of cooperation rather than competition and reap the rewards of teamwork.
Cons	Unless there is an incentive to populate it, content can become useless. Salespeople could see it as 'big brother' watching them or an administrative burden.

Success factors	Don't let it stop creative thinking.
	Not all insights are equally important, so get into the habit of getting experts to assess and prioritise them – perhaps using an Amazon-style star rating that reflects the value to others.
	Ensure lessons learned are easy to access and find.
	Avoid taking the easy option by using a previous solution, presentation or agenda without taking the time to consider whether it will really work.
How does it fit?	Sales process: It can significantly speed up all parts of the sales process. By choosing a previously used best practice, you can use 'cut and paste' where appropriate.
	Customer relationship: Use it for best practice for what works in customer interactions.
	Communication: It gives structure to communication between your salespeople, which is especially useful when some work remotely.
	Knowledge: It spreads knowledge and can bring the weakest salespeople up to the level of the best when structuring customer meetings, producing presentations and so on.

QUICK TIP **BUSINESS ENVIRONMENT**

Even if you lose a person to another job, make sure you keep their useful information. You could do this with your CRM system, customer account plans, key account management template or lessons-learned database.

4 Customer relationship management (CRM) software

What is it?	A customer relationship management system captures and displays a history of all interactions your company has had with a customer – meetings, telephone conversations, enquiries, orders, quotations, complaints, deliveries, invoices and payments.
Pros	It allows you to understand your customer more comprehensively, make better decisions and provide a better service.
Cons	It can be very time consuming to input data manually; so you run the risk of holding too much data, some of which is less important or even irrelevant.
	Watch the interface with the customer. You do not want them to feel that they are being 'watched', especially when they realise just how much information you have stored about them

Success factors

Major on the majors – focus on using the information to enhance the client relationship; don't get drowned in the detail.

Take care to ensure the accuracy of the data, and most importantly how up to date it is, because if either salespeople or customers question the accuracy they will simply ignore the system.

It is particularly useful if you can make the reports very visual, so you can easily see when orders are starting to reduce, or when customers switch to new products and services, or when the volume of complaints increases – without having to analyse rows and rows of figures.

Introduce the new system by identifying where your customer service is creaking. This will identify where the quick wins will come from and make sure that you deal with the key issues first.

In deciding what processes will be driven by CRM, take into account where the client records are now and how you will migrate them into the new system. The time that you migrate records is an excellent opportunity to improve the accuracy of your client data. Look as well at how the CRM system can link with your website.

Make sure you have a very senior sponsor; and, unless it is a simple system, a project manager is essential to ensure the system goes in on time, within budget and is meeting the objectives you set for it.

Don't forget the sales force and its attitude to admin. – use CRM to make the salespeople's job simpler not more complicated. The key to creating an effective CRM system is to start by being very clear about what you want it to do for you. This will have a big impact on the way you go about implementing it. Possible objectives are:

→ increased client retention;
→ more cross-selling and up-selling opportunities;
→ better campaign management;
→ better sales productivity;
→ better sales targeting.

How does it fit?

Sales process: Get the right people involved at the right time, depending on the interactions the customer has been having with you.

Customer relationship: It is possible to customise your interactions and the product or services you offer based on past history. You can use the information to help guide the customer in the choices or timings they make; you can also spot trends in their buying behaviour.

Communication: You can use the information to guide you as to the most appropriate time and the most appropriate way to be making contact.

Knowledge: You can gather information on all customer interactions and it can act as an early warning system for potential problems.

5 Key account management (KAM) template[1]

What is it?	A central repository of all information on key accounts that shows the status of your relationship and enables the gaining of new business and retention of existing business. This goes beyond the CRM system, which should be designed for the majority of customers.
Pros	It should make it easier for salespeople to develop a good strategic plan to maximise sales and profits from major customers in the long term.
	With the customer's input it can ensure that the sales team maximise sales and productivity and also produce demonstrable benefits to the customer's business.
	When used as a communication document it enables everyone involved in the account to work within the strategy and make sure that what they are doing and saying is within an agreed framework, no matter how remote they are or how little involvement they have with the customer. For example, it should make it very easy to brief a senior manager before a high-level meeting.
	Because it is a template it ensures that the sales team has covered all the bases and can make valid comparisons with other plans.
	It should help solidify the relationship with the customer and provide reference sites for use by the sales force.
	It makes handover when someone leaves the selling team much less problematical.
Cons	Setting up the template if done by a committee often makes the template too big and unwieldy for ease of use.
	Using the template can be quite a big job for the account manager and their team.
	Keeping it up to date can be seen as additional administration.
Success factors	Use a small team that includes at least one well respected account manager in it to set the template up. Also agree who is responsible for updating each section.
	When you publish it, publish an example at the same time.
	Ask yourself these questions:

- → What is its main objective?
- → Who must have access to it?
- → How often should each section be updated?
- → Does this drive account review meetings?

Don't make it so constricting that much of it is irrelevant to some account managers. Whenever you add content, think how you will use it. For example, templates often work well for normal companies but contain a lot of irrelevant material for public sector customers.

Make at least a part of it, perhaps the sales forecast, part of the account managers' normal duties so that they have to update the plan regularly.

---

[1] For more detail, see page 191 in Part D: Director's Toolkit.

How does it fit?

Sales process: It is a very valuable source of information for sub-account managers in different regions or countries to the account manager. It makes the discovery of opportunities around a customer's subsidiaries and divisions much quicker.

Customer relationship: Some people define the term 'working partnership' as one where 'the customer is involved in the supplier's planning process and vice versa'. This is the mechanism to make such a working partnership effective.

Communication: It shows anyone who needs access and is entitled to it exactly what the account manager's plan is.

Knowledge: It provides a thorough description of the customer, their history, competitors, strengths and weaknesses.

QUICK TIP **KEEP IT SIMPLE, STUPID**

Nowhere is the KISS mantra more important than in mandatory key account documentation.

---

6 The electronic pitch

What is it?

Using a webcast, video conferencing or interactive/collaborative websites to interact with your customer or your team.

Pros

Low cost and reducing the costs of travelling.

For internal meetings, agendas can be more focused and meetings can occur more frequently. If travel time is required, you often have to set up several meetings over two or three days to justify the cost of travel, whether you need that length of time or not.

Your customers do not always have time for face-to-face meetings, so using your website can be an effective way to demonstrate products or services during a phone conversation; you can even produce online presentations to go through together.

Cons

Not being able to 'relate' as well to individuals because you do not get physical feedback, such as body language, as well as in a face-to-face meeting.

Unreliable connections can interrupt a crucial virtual meeting.

Success factors

Make sure that using this technology is appropriate for the situation and for the customer. Do not try to force this on a customer for your convenience unless the customer doesn't justify expensive face-to-face meetings.

Measure the success of these meetings and change them if they are not effective.

	With your own team, make sure they still get valuable face-to-face time with you through one-to-one meetings or coaching sessions.
How does it fit?	Sales process: It can shorten the sales cycle as a result of more frequent and more focused meetings.
	Customer relationship: This can be enhanced due to the frequency of meetings, but be aware again that the quality of the interaction could suffer.
	Communication: Internally and externally this may be more appropriate and more frequent; however, face-to-face communication is replaced the quality could suffer.
	Knowledge: It can speed up knowledge transfer internally and enable you to transfer knowledge more frequently with your customer.

7 E-purchasing

What is it?	Customers soliciting prices and requesting specifications for goods and services electronically via e-auctions or electronic RFP (requests for proposal). More and more companies are making it possible for customers to 'serve themselves' electronically – for instance, purchasing directly on the supplier's website, checking the stock availability and tracking delivery dates.
Pros	The convenience and the time taken for the customer.
Cons	Internet auctions rarely allow the seller to find out how they position and/or design their product or service to match the customer's exact requirements and can force suppliers to compete only on price. This sounds great for the buyer, but often they choose the most aggressive supplier, not the supplier best able to meet their requirements. It's worth remembering that, particularly in buying complex solutions, companies get what they pay for.
Success factors	As a sales leader, develop a strategy so your team can maximise your return from e-auctions. It is low cost for you, so you may be prepared to sell old stock or low-cost services this way.
	Consider how e-purchasing will impact on your regular business.
	Be prepared for when existing customers switch to e-auctions; this may give your competitors a chance that they wouldn't have had through traditional channels.
	With e-RFPs anticipate when they are likely to arrive and ensure you have done the right amount of research and identification of requirements.
	Consider how you will differentiate yourself and demonstrate the value of your unique selling points.
	Help the prospect choose you based on factors other than just price.
	Make sure your website purchase system is very, very user friendly; it is worthwhile benchmarking against sites that you purchase from personally.

How does it fit?	Sales process: It can be a very efficient use of your sales resources, so don't be afraid to embrace this approach.
	Customer relationship: This also does little for customer relationships. You may choose to deal with these customers on a purely transactional basis, or find out before you enter an e-auction or complete an e-RFP how they want to be treated.
	Communication: This is low on communication, so you will need to compensate for this.
	Knowledge: Almost by definition e-auctions and e-RFPs will mean that you have not been able to gather sufficient knowledge to make your case, so as with communication have a method to compensate.

8 The sales pipeline scorecard

What is it?	An electronic method to measure your sales team – their activity, their level of knowledge, skills and their sales pipeline. The sales pipeline scorecard can also be used to improve electronic forecasting.
Pros	Easily accessible by all, it can identify improvements quickly. Results can be linked to what was done and how it was done.
	It makes measurement objective rather than subjective and can be very motivational.
	This can be standalone or linked to your CRM system.
	You can monitor actual performance against forecast.
Cons	If results start to deteriorate and salespeople are not managed through one-to-one meetings as well, it could end up being demotivating.
	If the data quality is questionable – 'garbage in, garbage out' – it will be useless.
Success factors	Make all the measurements objective, even if at first they appear purely subjective, such as knowledge and skills.
	In the pipeline include all parts of the sales process from selection criteria through to key account repeat orders.
	Use in conjunction with appraisals and one-to-one meetings.
How does it fit?	Sales process: There are clear measurements of each salesperson's effectiveness at every stage of the sales process.
	Customer relationship: The pipeline scorecard will ensure that the right prospects are chosen and that the customer is receiving the right attention at all stages of the sales process.
	Communication: It provides a standard way to communicate what is working and what needs addressing. No member of the team can say that they are being 'picked on'.
	Knowledge: As an objective measure of your sales team's knowledge, it is easy to identify knowledge gaps and put plans in place to fill those gaps and measure the results.

9 The virtual team

What is it?
Online forums, chatrooms, web seminars.

Pros
You have the ability to share information with a wide audience of people who you don't necessarily know.
The information is always available and reasonably low cost.
It can generate very good quality insight, information and answers to problems or situations.

Cons
Answers may not always be accurate.
You need to understand people's own agendas.

Success factors
Use these technologies as part of a 'mix'; do not rely solely on this method.

How does it fit?
Customer relationship: It can provide solutions to your customers that you couldn't have come up with internally. It can be a valuable input to after-sales service as people input their experience with your products.
Communication: A quick, low-cost and effective way to communicate with peers, your team and your customers.
Knowledge: A very effective way to build your own knowledge, maintaining a clear focus.

10 The virtual office

What is it?
The ability to work anywhere in the world (home, hotels airports, service stations) and operate as if you were in your own office by using mobile phones, PDAs (personal digital assistants) and wireless laptops.

Pros
Sales leaders are always available for their team and their customers.
It reduces time in the office and increases time spent in actual selling.
You can use 'down time' productively.

Cons
You have less face-to-face time with your salespeople.
By always being available it can be difficult to switch off, which can lead to stress.
For the salesperson, it can make the job very lonely.

Success factors
Be aware that your team still need face-to-face time; this makes one-to-one and team meetings vital.
Spot warning signs that this is affecting motivation and performance.

How does it fit?
Sales process: More time in front of customers should shorten the sales cycle.
Customer relationship: The customer knows that you are always available.
Communication: This is more regular but of lower quality than face-to-face communication.
Knowledge: It gives you more opportunity to gather and access knowledge, especially at the last minute.

Some conclusions

Technology is developing so fast that it is impossible to predict how it could impact sales in the future, but we must embrace it and use it wisely. Look for ways that you can:

→ take away or reduce mundane tasks;

→ increase the speed at which things get done;

→ use freed-up time as more selling time;

→ use technology to display information in multiple ways, getting the right information to the right people at the right time;

→ improve the accuracy of records and administration;

→ use technology to improve the customer experience;

→ increase the support you give your sales team from initiation to delivery.

QUICK TIP **MAKE IT SALESPERSON FRIENDLY**
Develop systems that are easy for all salespeople to use, not just those who love computers.

At the same time, avoid the pitfalls, such as:

→ a feeling that 'big brother' is watching us;

→ massive opportunities for technology-based fraud (don't think this can only happen to someone else, it could happen to you);

→ relying on information on the internet, which is notorious for not being accurate or up to date;

→ losing touch with the softer part of sales – the key relation-ships between team members and key stakeholders including customers;

→ overloading people with information through a desire to display it in too many ways;

→ falling foul of current and new legislation – there are various rules and regulations, such as the Data Protection Act, so make sure someone checks that you are within the law, particularly if you are using email lists to find prospects;

→ the competition finding out too much about you because you have made information available to the people you really want to have it.

STOP – THINK – ACT

Now stop. Before going out and investing in the latest and greatest, remember that technology is just an enabler. Success will ultimately depend on your ability to lead your team, your behaviours and how you interact with others. Be wary of being drawn into new technologies too quickly – let someone else make the mistakes, but then learn quickly. Finally, if you do decide to introduce new systems into your team, think carefully about the possible risks – what could go wrong?

Ask yourself and your team these questions:

What should we do?	What technologies are available that will help to improve effectiveness and efficiency?
Who do we need to involve?	Who would benefit and why?
What resources will we require?	What level of investment would be required?
What is the timing?	When would be a good time to introduce the new technology – is there is a 'window of opportunity'?

Visit **www.Fast-Track-Me.com** to use the Fast Track online planning tool.

Using emotion in selling
Geoff King

Mankind are governed more by their feelings than by reason. (Samuel Adams (1722–1803) American patriot and politician)

In selling, as in so much of life, a high emotional intelligence can be more useful to you than a person with a high IQ.

People buy from people they like

Being personable is a huge advantage in selling. People don't buy from companies; they buy from people. That means that whenever they can, they will buy from someone they like and trust.

In nearly all sales it is emotion, not logic, that persuades people to buy. (What usually happens is that people buy on emotional grounds and then justify their decision on logical grounds.) Logic on its own has very little persuasive power. You should speak more to their heart than to their head. The only real exception to this rule occurs when people buy commodities.

You need to act honestly

The best successes occur when you build lasting relationships with customers who grow to trust and rely on you. It is one reason why the best salespeople do not come across as salespeople.

Looking at the figure opposite, you may well have met people who sell towards the right-hand side of this spectrum and you probably didn't like them. So why do they sell like that? Well, a few of them would have done it because they lacked a conscience. (Psychologists believe this condition affects about 1 per cent of the general population.) However, the overwhelming majority would have done so to defer awkward problems until a later date. It is a very human trap to fall into, and one you need to avoid.

You need to be here

Overly honest   Honest   Exaggerating   Bending the truth   Lying

◄──── Politician ────►

◄──── Estate agent ────►

◄──── Fraudster ────►

'Your bum looks   'This government's   'I did not have
  big in that'   policies have been   sexual relations with
                           a success'   that woman'

So how do you create charm?

As with so many things, Shakespeare summed up the essence of charm better than anyone before or since. Specifically he said that charm most frequently occurs when a person is 'kind and courteous' in equal measure. Nowadays we might express that as when integrity and *savoir faire* are equally balanced in a person's character. Too much integrity makes us seem blunt; too much *savoir faire* makes us seem slippery. People with both qualities balanced, and present in reasonable quantities, are the ones best able to charm. But how should they use charm?

Focus the emotion in the right area

Sales conversations fall into one of the following three types.

1 **Personal/personal conversations.** These conversations just focus on personal issues and have nothing to do with business. They are conversations about the news, recent sports events, the weather and such like. In business, this type of conversation often happens when you first meet someone, and there is a place for it at that point. It will not, however, go far to increasing your sales.

2 **Business/business conversations.** These conversations are the exact opposite. They are essentially impersonal conversations about business issues. They are conversations along the lines of, 'So, Mr Customer, how would this proposed development affect the company?'

3 **Business/personal conversations.** These conversations sound at first glance to be similar to business/business conversations but

there is a subtle difference. Usually, they take one of two slightly different forms. The first form asks how your prospect *feels* about something. For example, 'So, Mr Customer, how do you feel this proposed development will affect the company?' The second form is slightly stronger. It asks how something will *affect them personally*. Typically, it will be a question such as, 'So, Mr Customer, how will the proposed development affect your own situation here?' In both cases the question is directed at the emotions the prospect feels about his business world.

The key to using emotion in selling is to focus on the business/personal. It will aid the consultative approach and will help you gain trust. The prospect will see you not just as 'another consultant' but as someone who is 'focused on them'. They may well perceive this subconsciously, but they will perceive it.

Business/personal conversations are also more likely to uncover real buying motives. In contrast, a business/business approach is more likely to get a 'standard' response.

One final note. Avoid the trap of asking, 'How does *the company* feel about this?' Instead say, 'How do *you* feel about this?' Asking how the company feels about things will get you the standard response.

So what are the emotions behind buying decisions?

The rational part of the buyer will think about the reasons for buying, but at the same time emotion will flow over those thoughts. We already know that people buy on emotional grounds and then justify their decision on logical grounds. What we should also know is that those emotions are capable of very powerful effects. But exactly which emotions are at work here?

There is of course a wide sea of emotions but by far the most powerful ones, from the point of view of selling, are fear and greed. They can be so powerful as to leave rationality bobbing like a cork upon them.

Yet despite their power, you should never use fear or greed to sell. If you try, the prospect will see what you are doing and dislike you for it. What you must do, however, is be respectful of these two emotions because they are usually present and they are usually powerful. That way, you will have some empathy with your prospect.

Fear of loss and desire for gain

But which emotion, fear or greed, is the more powerful? In reality they are two sides of the same coin. Most people fear loss more than they desire gain. If you give a group of people a 50:50 chance – for example, a chance to gain £2,000 or to lose £2,000 – most of the group will choose not to play. They fear the loss more than they desire the gain. Shakespeare also summed up this emotion rather well. He wrote that: 'Things of like value, differing in their owners, are prized by their masters.' What it means is we tend to value something we already own more than something we could own. It is a type of inertia.

Using emotion to sell

So far, we have just looked at how emotion affects the buyer. But can the seller use their own emotions to help with the selling? The answer, perhaps surprisingly, is not that much. True, emotion can help with certain parts of selling. In negotiation, for instance, or motivation, or in the enthusiasm you show when selling to a socialite. But showing emotion per se is of little use. For example, most people value the financial advice of a staid bank manager over that of an exuberant free thinker even when both of those people give the same advice. The reason is that the bank manager appears the safer option of the two. A conservative image is usually a safe bet when selling.

There is, however, one area of emotion that is tremendously useful for the seller – *intuition*. Nowadays we are conditioned to believe that information uncovered by science is of better quality than information uncovered by our own senses. But is that really true? Your senses are the result of several million years' testing in a harsh environment. By contrast there is a close association between things labelled 'technology' and things that do not work. Most people have strong intuition if they would but use it.

But, of course, emotion is not just about what you say. It is about how you appear too.

IMPLEMENTING CHANGE

It may be a cliché, but we live in a fast-paced world and change is the norm. The sales function is no exception. If we compare selling now with 20 years ago the role is completely different. We rarely see the slick fast-talking salesperson; instead we meet confident, educated and sophisticated people who truly want to understand the customer and produce long-lasting solutions. The changes are driven by the market and how the customers have developed. If we only do what we did last year, we will get the results we got last year and that's just not good enough. So with the demand for improved results year on year, we are bound to see further change in the future.

To be an effective sales manager you must not only be able to embrace change but also be able to lead change.

QUICK TIP **TAKE IT STEP BY STEP**
Break down major changes into manageable steps.

Planning for change

What drives change?

For sales there are two main drivers of change:

→ changes in the marketplace;

→ internal company changes of strategy, products, services, technologies and processes.

Changes in the marketplace

→ **Customers need to increase their sales and improve margins.** At the same time, they are under pressure to improve customer retention and their speed of response. Strategically they have to differentiate in order to improve market share and probably launch new products and services. They have to develop new ways to sell by using more inside sales or the internet. Their demands for you to change could also be due to their actual experience or their perceptions of you as a supplier. They may have seen real or perceived deterioration in service levels or in the range and quality of the products and services you offer.

→ **Competitors force you to continuously consider how you operate; you are in a real competition that never ends.** At no stage can you consider yourself the winner because someone will come back at you very quickly. But there are losers and they are often those who cannot change quickly and effectively enough. Don't forget that your competitors have the same aspirations as you, so they are also aiming to increase sales, improve margins, improve customer retention and so on. So if their reduced costs are passed on to customers in the form of lower prices, you have to find similar savings just to stand still. A publisher that I know had to make a dramatic reduction in the cost of producing books. Up until then they had stayed loyal to the UK printing trade, unlike many competitors who had moved production abroad. Faced with such a dramatic problem they went to their suppliers and simply told them that if they did not decrease their prices by 25 per cent they would go abroad, despite the problems that would cause. Guess what? – they found the necessary savings pretty quickly. In this case the savings had a direct impact on the printers' profit margins. It would have been relatively easy to have predicted the publisher would be looking to move production to a low-cost country, so they should have been proactive in finding the cost savings in advance of the customer pressure, instead of reacting to events and panicking. You could also be up against new competitors. Mergers and acquisitions are creating more powerful ones while others may drop out of the market – all these could be a catalyst for you to change.

Internal company changes of strategy, products and processes

→ These may arise from the **company's overall strategy**: the need to grow organically by 25 per cent per year, to enter new markets, reduce staff levels, increase automation and so on; board strategies change much faster now than they did in the past.

→ **Shareholders** are demanding innovation, improved profits, dramatic growth through mergers/acquisitions and are driven by the need to protect the company's long-term sustainability.

→ Your **department's objectives** will change in line with the aspirations and strategy of the company and your division.

→ And, of course, your own **career objectives** and work-life balance aspirations will also change with your and the company's circumstances.

What types of change are there?

In sales we can change proactively or reactively. Whilst being proactive tends to be seen as more favourable than having to react to changing circumstances, this is only really the case if the changes are necessary and well managed. Be careful that the change you are considering is not just cosmetic or ego-led. People question the old adage 'If it ain't broke don't fix it' but I tend to agree with it. After all, we have so much to do to improve our professionalism as it is, without worrying about areas that are working fine. Don't forget that if you decide to make changes to fore-stall a threat, someone in your team will resist the change, preferring to do things the way they always have.

As a sales leader you are going to have to lead the team through a number of change processes. It is highly likely that the sales and other processes that you want to see in place are not there to start with. That is why it is so important to think about managing change successfully.

When you react to external pressure it is because the alternative is to continue as is and suffer the consequences – this gives us no choice but to react. Often these changes can be very successful because it is easier to get people's buy-in, as it is obvious to all why the change is needed and what the consequence of inaction is. Those involved can view this external influence as a 'common enemy' so there is less need to create buy-in.

 QUICK TIP **SPELL OUT THE BENEFITS**
Even where the change is forced upon the team, make the benefits of changing clear, rather than just talking about avoiding a problem.

Change within your sales framework

Once you have realised the need to change, think carefully, about exactly why you need to change and whether the changes required are internally or externally driven. What do you want to get from the change? What are your objectives, what will be the results and the payback of the change, and, finally, how will you ensure the change happens? Keep challenging yourself to ensure that it is not just change for the sake of change.

The first place you will be looking to make changes will be your results. Therefore, your objectives could be to:

→ improve revenue;

→ increase margins;

→ secure future growth;

→ improve customer retention;

→ improve efficiencies.

To achieve these objectives, concentrate on a number of areas in your sales framework to make changes.

How can you use change to improve your team's effectiveness?

Analyse how the team spend their day: the percentage of their time spent on customer-facing activities and the types of customers they are dealing with. Make sure that they are spending their time with the right customers and prospects. You will have to think about:

→ potential spend;

→ profitability;

→ fit with other business;

→ conversion rates of prospects to buyers;

→ products and services they choose to sell.

Now look at the salespeople's level of motivation to stretch themselves and gauge their drive to be more successful. Analyse the quality of the interactions they have with their customers in terms of the influence they are exerting, measured by closing ratios and customer retention levels. Finally, check their skills, knowledge, sales planning and use of the sales process.

You may need to think about changing your leadership style. Make sure that the sales compensation scheme works to assist you to make changes. Even if a compensation scheme has worked in one environment, you will probably have to consider changing it to reflect your new way of doing things.

What can you do to optimise the pipeline?

The way you manage the pipeline will have a direct impact on your results. Again, check the type of customer and prospects. You can gain efficiencies by looking at where customers are located geographically –

the closer together they are, the easier for a salesperson to visit a number in one day. You may be able to gain effectiveness by concentrating each salesperson on one industry or sector. Their industry knowledge gained in one customer area will be useful in another. Then there are the issues of turnover or number of employees. Think it through for your own situation. In the end the choice should be towards customers who will bring you the best long-term profit.

QUICK TIP **REWARD PIPELINE GROWTH**
If finding new customers is vital to making budget, consider a reward scheme for regular prospecting.

In your pipeline you may need to change your selection criteria, the way you develop suspects to prospects or prospects to buying customers, or how you look after your buying customers.

Make sure your team structure, sales processes and support staff reinforce your pipeline activities. There may be a way that your CRM system could be more effective in passing leads to salespeople, and the same goes for your customer service people. Could you think about expanding your way to market – e.g. via the internet or through agents? Are your sales processes appropriate and do your people find value in the processes, particularly those that you have recently introduced, and are they following them correctly? Are you optimising your use of the technology that is available to support pipeline activities? Finally, ask yourself how you are cooperating with marketing. It may be possible to improve the pipeline by developing joint strategies or joint campaigns.

How can you take advantage of market trends?

You may need to consider how you can use your monitoring processes to identify opportunities and threats, and take the appropriate action.

An effective way to look at the market is by using the PESTEL model. (This stands for political change, economic trends, social trends, technological change, environmental change and legal changes.) This can also be used to help identify where to look for opportunities and threats that could drive a change in your approach.

→ Political change – such as a change in government and their poli-cies, which could require you to change how and what you sell.

→ Economic trends – such as changes in consumer confidence or disposable income.

→ Social trends – such as smoking, fitness, more leisure time or an ageing population.

→ Technological change – such as the use of mobile phones, shrinking size of appliances and increased computing power.

→ Environmental change – such as the need to switch away from fossil fuels, or deforestation.

→ Legal changes – such as mass marketing laws, licensing laws or drivers' hours.

Market drivers can also include globalisation, changes in commodity prices, the availability of resources, new sources of raw material or labour, or alternative resources. All these could increase or decrease the demand for your products or services.

What will 'good' look like?

→ **Think about the destination: where you want to end up and what 'good' will look like.** Having a powerful vision can help, not only with where you are headed, but also with the communication and planning.

→ **Get quick wins.** Early in the change process, identify what they are and how they help.

→ **Anticipate problems and dissenters.** Put a plan in place to reduce the impact or address them when they happen.

→ **Decide who you want to get involved and why.** Have a plan for how you will get them on board, and understand the impact this may have on their regular job and those of others.

→ **Think about motivation.** How will you motivate all those involved and affected by the process and the resulting change?

→ **How will you embed the change?** Often the fun part is initiating the change but, especially for salespeople, once the fun part is over we walk away and the change doesn't stick.

How will everyone know what you want to achieve and how you will achieve it?

→ **Communicate well and often.** Your communication plan depends on the extent of the change you are trying to make. Communication to a large audience may involve 'town hall' meetings (where you address a large group, usually all the employees at one location), newsletters, road shows, one-on-ones, presentations and workgroups. For small changes, it will be less formal, but it is just as important that it happens. Make sure you involve everyone affected by the change. Suppose, for example, you are changing the key account management system to bring in a senior manager as a sponsor for each key account. You need to inform everyone involved in the account, from the sales team to the maintenance engineers and their managers, so that people start to channel information to the appropriate sponsor.

→ **When you communicate, check for understanding by seeking feedback (honest feedback) – people don't always 'hear' what was said.** Especially during the change process, people often interpret the communication the way they would like it to be, or are selective in their hearing because they are being defensive and resisting the change.

→ **People are people so adjust your communication style and medium to the needs of individuals.** Some people react much better to a telephone call than to an email, for instance.

→ **Use your vision for how things are going to be to explain the situation in a simple way.** It is important to keep the communication consistent. Be honest and explain the objectives and the benefits of what you are trying to do.

QUICK TIP **COVER THE BASES**

Whenever you communicate about change, always remind people of the benefits to them personally, the team and the organisation.

CASE STORY **TELECOMMUNICATIONS, ANGELA'S STORY**

Narrator Angela is a very successful salesperson in the telecommunications industry. She always wanted career progression and was very keen to move up when a more senior position became available. However, she needed someone else to help her see that moving up isn't always the secret to success.

Context The fast-changing telecommunications industry has very short product life cycles. In this company the salespeople who made a first sale kept that customer and then attempted to grow the account.

Issue Angela, was very successful in finding new customers and making the first sale. It was not always the most profitable sale but it brought new customers in. She then tried to expand business to that customer by proposing solutions that the current product set really struggled to fulfil. The company either lost customer satisfaction by failing to deliver what had been promised or lost money adapting products to meet the specification. The support manager responsible for satisfying customers tried to make Angela keep within guidelines but found it very difficult to retain her attention while he explained the problem, so he then tried to make her use a process to get permission to propose any new solutions.

Solution A new sales director decided to differentiate between new-business salespeople and account developers. He put Angela and others in with the new-business team and made sure that their bonus scheme did not reduce their expected earnings if they concentrated on bringing in new customers.

Learning Salespeople naturally divide into 'hunters' and 'farmers'. Hunters are those who enjoy the challenge of making a lot of cold calls, wresting people away from their current suppliers and moving on. They have short attention spans and spend as little time as possible on getting the order. Farmers enjoy building a relationship with a customer, really understanding their business and carefully marrying the capabilities of their product set with the opportunities offered by customer demand.

So what are the potential pitfalls?

→ **In general salespeople like to be challenged and actually seek change, but they tend to resist when change is 'done' to them.** They resist when it changes them, puts them into their stretch or panic zone and makes them lose trust or feel helpless.

→ **People will always have reasons not to change.** It is important to identify what these are and seek ways to reduce them. A default is often, 'That's the way it has always been done here' or 'Better the devil you know.' I am sure you have heard them all at some time!

→ **Some people will continue to want to react rather than be proactive.** There can be many reasons for this – some people just don't like autonomy or responsibility, they like their job to be defined by incoming demands. Not everyone is going to be like you, so think best how to manage this.

→ **While you are talking about change and being persuasive, be aware that people's stated objections may not be their real ones.** You need to get to understand the real resistance to change; it could be in your approach.

→ **Be aware that people may make assumptions about your motivation to change.** They may think that you are just trying to prove yourself, or that this is just part of a plan to reduce the workforce. Try to find out what these assumptions are and clarify the situation.

→ **Resources may not be available at the time you had planned to have them.** Analyse how you can change the plan so that the overall timescale is not affected, or look at other resources; be careful to spot these kind of issues early.

→ **Don't lose momentum.** You will get the occasional setback because it is often a lot harder or more complex than you first thought. If you are sure the changes you have initiated are right, regroup, understand why it is taking longer and get back on the case.

→ **Sometimes it is difficult just managing the large number of people who need to be involved.** For example, a person you are relying on is getting the tasks done but taking much longer than was expected. Do you change the plan or bring in someone else to speed things up? You may have to consider breaking the job down and seeking help from your champions and mentors.

→ **Look at yourself for potential traps.** Perhaps the change initiative was not well enough considered, or perhaps for cultural or timing reasons the change just wasn't appropriate.

→ **Beware of 'scope creep'.** If the plan hasn't been fully considered, or the measurements aren't in place, it is easy for a change initiative to become far bigger than first intended; the more people involved the more likely this is to happen. There will be occasions when it could be right to expand the change initiative, but consider it as a new project and go back to the drawing board to check what resources will now be necessary and how the timescale will be affected.

→ **If the results are not as great as you expected consider your next step.** If, for example, you have rolled out a pilot and it is not producing the same level of financial benefits as had been planned, do you cut costs or search for a way of improving performance?

How to make sure change happens

Make a plan to include milestones and deadlines. Decide on the resources required. Who will you involve and what will their role be? Identify allies and detractors. Try to see it from their point of view by working out what is in it for them. Make adjustments if the truthful answer to the question is nothing. Consider brainstorming sessions and get a group to come up with the ideal solution. Decide how to build their ideas into your plan and be sure to communicate back to the group how you used their ideas.

If the change is major – for example, you are implementing an activity monitoring system – make sure you have the big battalions behind you. Early on you will need to identify a champion and mentors to ensure that the initiative is endorsed and maintained from the top down. You win high-level support by having a credible plan and communicating the benefits and foreseeable hurdles well. Be clear about what you want, but also be prepared to be flexible if the situation changes or if others have better ideas on how to change or implement plans. Be careful not to be too impatient; you may be weeks or months ahead of others, so do give people time to adjust. Consider all the impacts and effects the changes will have – positive and negative.

In terms of the budget, estimate the cost and the benefits (costs could be people's time, IT, materials, consultants, training, communication, research).

Give some thought to potential risks. For instance:

→ systems not working on time;

→ some people refusing to adopt the new approach;

→ late implementation because the time involved to learn new processes, skills and product/service details is longer than expected;

→ people who support the change all the time it is going well then walk away when things go wrong – the results could be lost customers or staff leaving.

You will need to start to prioritise tasks. You may also need to turn to consultants if the change is significant, since they can bring expertise that is not available within the company.

Have a change management process – this will include monitoring and measurement systems. Think about how you will introduce corrective measures if it goes off track. You may want to track it in an electronic format; you will almost certainly find it worthwhile drawing a Gantt chart for the project, no matter how simple or complicated the change is. You can choose your own references, but use these headings as a guide: task, duration and relationship (see figure opposite). If the project is complicated you will be looking at weeks rather than days.

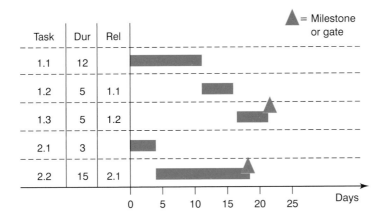

You may want to invest time in investigating how your company has managed change in the past; there may be systems, processes and people that can help. Also check what has worked in the past (use the lessons-learned database) and identify what hasn't worked and why.

The plan and management process will need to be appropriate to the scale of the project. Think about the three Ps that you will need to manage: **plan** (tasks and timings), **people** (keeping the key people motivated and on track) and **performance** (the project objectives). Keep your focus balanced on all three.

The plan-do-check-act (PDCA) cycle is a continuous improvement approach to managing a project or team (see figure overleaf).

1 **Plan.** You have to plan your activities (you will have done this already if you have a Gantt chart).

2 **Do.** This implies completing the activities necessary for success.

3 **Check.** You need to check the progress you're making towards implementing the plan. This will reveal any problems in any of the three areas concerned.

4 **Act.** Make decisions that will bring the project back on track by resolving the problems.

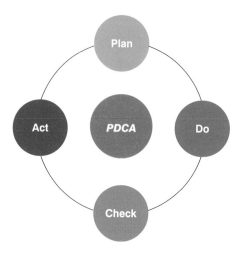

How do we stay flexible?

Whilst you need to understand the principles of planning and performance monitoring, you also need to be flexible and responsive to the team and how things are going. Think about how tight or loose your controls really need to be. Too loose and you run the risk of missing deadlines and going off at a tangent, but too tight and there is danger of demotivating those involved.

Nowhere is this tight versus loose leadership style more visible than when a team leader or change project manager gets bogged down by the project management side. There may be instances where you can afford non-critical activities to slip a bit and they won't compromise the end date. If you insist that every task is done exactly on time and lose sight of the big picture, you risk affecting the creativity of the team and can create motivation problems by an unhealthy concentration on the tasks as you planned them. It is common when a project manager is so intent on ticking off the activities that people ignore shortcuts and better ways of doing things just to keep the manager happy.

QUICK TIP **PLAN FOR THE UNKNOWN**
Keep in mind that you are probably going to have to change the plan frequently, so do build flexibility into it from the beginning.

STOP – THINK – ACT

At the end of this chapter you will be aware that creating the vision or identifying areas for improvement can often be the straightforward part. It is implementing these initiatives that is not necessarily quick or easy. They need to be planned and implemented using a disciplined approach. Use the team audit on page 20 and the team sales management audit on page 183 to identify the gaps in your current approach to selling. Then identify what you will need to do to make it happen.

What should we do?	What stages and tasks are appropriate?
Who do we need to involve?	Who needs to be involved and why?
What resources will we require?	What information, facilities, materials, equipment or budget will be required?
What is the timing?	How long will each activity typically take?

Visit **www.Fast-Track-Me.com** to use the Fast Track online planning tool.

Sales management in the ascendency

Professor John Roberts

In the first half of the twentieth century most marketing activity consisted of sales. At IBM, there was an adage that it was impossible to get to the very top unless one had 'carried a bag' (been a salesperson). While this emphasis persisted in most business-to-business (B2B) markets after the Second World War, consumer marketing (B2C) soon became enamoured with marketing in terms of mass communications, product design and other functions more distant to the customer than closing the sale.

To understand this trend it is useful to consider the respective functions of marketing and sales. The activities of the firm may be described by the brands it develops and the products and services that are marketed under the umbrella of those brands. That is, we can think of the firm in terms of the products in the columns in the figure overleaf. An alternative approach is to think of the firm in terms of its potential customers (or groups of customers segmented by application, geography, etc.) whose needs the firms hope to meet. These are depicted in the rows of the matrix. This product–market matrix is used for a variety of purposes in business planning. For example, Igor Ansoff used it to classify growth opportunities into those arising from existing products or new products and from existing markets or new markets.

MARKETING
Brands, products:
using advertising, production, etc.

Products

		A	B	C	D	E
	1	X		X	X	
	2		X	X		
	3	X		X	X	
	4					X
	5	X	X	X	X	X

SALES — Customers, accounts: using service and account management, etc. — Customers

Of course, the two approaches are complementary. A firm cannot exist, no matter how good its products and services, without customers to whom to sell them. Similarly, no matter how loyal a firm's installed customer base, it will not make money unless it can find products and services to address their unmet needs. We gain different insights from cutting the matrix by column or by row, and indeed sometimes we need to be more granular and analyse it at the cell level (for example, for niche products).

What then caused marketing to gain its ascendency in B2C markets after the Second World War? Firstly, there was an excess of demand with many shortages following the war, meaning that closing the sale provided less leverage than in a demand-driven market. Secondly, wages started increasing dramatically after the war, meaning that the traditional sales model only made sense for high cost items. While the *Encyclopaedia Britannica* salesperson could justify a call to sell a $2000 set of books, the milkman soon disappeared. Thirdly, mass media had an explosion. The pre-war growth in radio was soon swamped by the much more effective medium of television, giving manufacturers enormous reach with effective but undifferentiated communications. Mass media was complemented by an even stronger trend towards mass production. It was this environment into which Procter & Gamble introduced the concept of brand management, on the basis that by focusing on the columns of the above diagram a manufacturer could gain considerable economies of scale and create strong barriers to entry with effective branding. Marketing became the key customer-facing strategic function and sales was seen as more operational.

This situation persisted for most of the remainder of the twentieth century. However, we are now seeing a return to an emphasis on sales. While this has largely been the case in B2B markets all along, B2C markets are also seeing a renewed emphasis on understanding and addressing customer needs, by using the rows to work out the requisite columns, rather focusing on the columns and working out the rows to which they should be applied. The question obviously arises as to the trends that are driving this change. That will dictate how far we can expect the pendulum to swing.

Before I address that issue, it is worth pointing out that (to the extent that sales represents understanding the customer's needs and developing a product to meet them, while marketing consists of taking products and services and finding markets that will value them) sales is a much better reflection of the customer orientation than marketing. It is difficult for customer-facing staff not to be customer oriented, when the customer is busy making sure that the staff understand their problems.

So, why the swing back to sales? There are many reasons for sales' new ascendency. Firstly, we have moved away from an economy based on scarcity, and so demand can no longer be taken for granted. It must be discovered, catered to and fulfilled. The deal must be closed and that is now harder. The move to solution selling has been largely a reflection of this. IBM's customers got sick and tired of being talked to by the Hardware Division, the Software Division and the General Services Division. They wanted a solution to their problem. George Day of the Wharton School has described the pain that this has caused organisations as they have had to reorganise from a product line basis to a market segment one.

Secondly, mass media began to fragment. With this fragmentation of the audience it became possible, and then necessary, to address one's different segments in different ways. The heavy hand of communications' economies of scale no longer trumped the welfare and profit benefits from catering to heterogeneous needs. With digitisation, it became cost effective to address huge numbers of different segments in different ways. Tesco found that it could greatly increase profits by talking to four million different segments differently. While the salesperson was still prohibitively expensive for all but the most expensive products or services, selling could now be automated. Blattberg and Deighton's work[1] gives a nice description of the addressable customer. The information advantage has been a major key in the trend towards sales.

[1] Blattberg, R. and Deighton, J. (1991) 'Interactive marketing: exploiting the age of addressability', *Sloan Management Review,* 33 (1), 5–14.

Thirdly, the fulfilment of meeting heterogeneous needs was also becoming cheaper. Computer aided design (CAD) and manufacture (CAM) now means that it is profitable to provide different products for different groups, increasing the requirement to understand those needs and differentially deliver to them, using sales.

Finally, channel rationalisation has meant that either the brand owner is closer to the consumer (as is the case with store brands such as Aldi, Sainsbury's, or Tesco's Finest), or the customer (the retailer) has so much market power relative to the consumer (the shopper) that much more of the leverage for a consumer marketer comes from its B2B function than its B2C function.

We have returned to where the customer is king again, and so the person closest to them, the salesperson, is a highly valued member of court. It is hard to see a trend on the horizon that will cause the pendulum to swing back in the near term.

CAREER
FAST TRACK

Whatever you have decided to do in terms of developing your career as a manager, to be successful you need to take control, plan ahead and focus on the things that will really make a difference. You need to ask yourself how you get into your company's key talent pool.

The first ten weeks of a new role will be critical. Get them right and you will be off to a flying start and will probably succeed. Get them wrong and you will come under pressure and even risk being moved on rather quickly. Plan this initial period to make sure you are not overwhelmed by the inevitable mass of detail that will assail you on arrival. Make sure that other people's priorities do not put you off the course that you have set yourself.

Once you have successfully eased yourself into your new role as a sales leader and gained the trust of your boss and the team, start to make things happen. Firstly, focus on your leadership style and how it needs to change to suit the new role; then focus on the team. Are they the right people and, if so, what will make them work more effectively as a sales team?

Finally, at the appropriate time, you need to think about your next career move, and whether you are interested in getting to the top and becoming a company director. It is not for everyone, as the commitment, time and associated stress can be offputting, but the sense of responsibility and leadership can be enormously rewarding.

You've concentrated on performance up until now – now it's time to look at your Fast Track career.

THE FIRST TEN WEEKS

The first ten weeks as a new sales manager or team leader are absolutely critical. The spotlight will be on you, so don't get into a position where your weaknesses are exposed, but concentrate on ensuring that your strengths shine through. This chapter gives you a step-by-step guide on how to navigate your way through those important first weeks in your new role. After all, you cannot 'press rewind' if you get it wrong. To take control, the Fast Track manager will seek to get hold of key facts, build relationships and develop simple mechanisms for monitoring and control – establishing or confirming simple but effective team processes.

Changing roles

Why is this a critical time?

Whenever you start a new role or job, whether within your existing business or joining a new company, you have an opportunity to make a positive impression on others. However, recognise that you will only get one chance to make a first impression[1] – get the first few months wrong and it could impact your relationships with others for a very long time.

During a period of transition, the team you will be joining will have few preconceptions. People will typically have an open mind and be willing to

[1]Watkins, Michael (2003), *The First 90 Days*, Boston MA: Harvard Business School Press.

try new ideas, giving you the benefit of the doubt. We often see this phe-nomenon when consultants are called in to resolve a critical business issue. They often say exactly the same things as some of the internal managers, but as outsiders their views are respected and acted upon.

This is typically a period of high emotional energy and activities will often get a higher level of enthusiasm and commitment. Use this time wisely and you will gain significant advantage.

What are the potential pitfalls?

Whilst this period of transition presents opportunities to make a good impression, take care not to get it wrong. Few people recover from a bad start in a new role. You will be faced with a number of challenges to overcome.

→ You will lack knowledge and expertise in your new role and this will make you vulnerable to getting decisions wrong.

→ In every team there will be a mixture of people and politics – getting in with the wrong people can limit your opportunities for future promotion.

→ There will be a lot to do in a short period of time and you may well feel overwhelmed by it all.

→ Most effective managers rely heavily on their informal networks, but in the early stages of a new job these don't exist

What is the worst-case scenario?

You will probably find that in the first few weeks everything will go well, that people give you the benefit of the doubt: normally they will forgive any mistakes because you are new to the role. However, this soon changes. They are looking at you closely and in the end will expect you to perform like any other manager.

During this initial period, it is vital that you take the steps necessary to set yourself up for longer-term success, or else you run the risk of falling into the 'chasm'[2] – you make a good start but then people begin to see

[2] Moore, Geoffrey A. (1999 revised edition), *Crossing the Chasm*, New York: HarperBusiness.

what you are doing as just 'bog standard'. Plan your first ten weeks carefully in order to set yourself up for longer-term success. The figure below identifies the need to demonstrate tangible results early on or risk failure shortly after your 'honeymoon period' has ended.

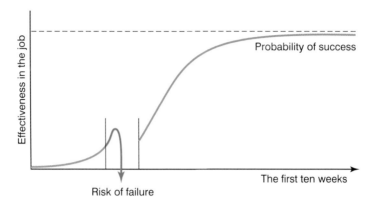

 CASE STORY *CAR FLEET SALES OPERATION, ALAN'S STORY*

Narrator Alan had a long career in front-line sales. Selling cars of the same make in a showroom, he had realised that relationships were vital. However, he understood that developing a close relationship with one person could often limit access to other decision makers.

Context Alan had recently joined a car fleet sales team as a first-line manager. He took over a team that included a number of very experienced salespeople.

Issue Whilst the team had a very good track record of making budget, Alan found that their sales forecasts were very poor in terms of expected order dates. The weekly sales forecasts included deals that had simply been shifted from the previous week. Investigating the lack of accuracy in meeting order dates, Alan discovered that the salespeople had very limited contacts – often they were focusing on the purchasing people with whom they had been dealing for a number of years. In one case the purchasing manager would tell the salesperson that he was in a position to sign. However, after the company's weekly management meeting he would change his mind and say that the management had decided that the order would have to be postponed because budget had to be spent on raw materials or marketing.

Solution Alan did a close investigation of this one customer and found that the decision-making process included a finance manager and a human resources manager as well as the purchasing manager. He helped the salesperson to expand their contacts in the company without losing the support of the purchasing manager. By talking to all three people the salesperson was able to produce much more accurate timings for sales.

Learning In big purchasing decisions it is very rare for one person to have total control. Make sure you know how the decision will be made and who will be involved.

The first ten weeks

What should I do before I start?

In the first ten weeks, be prepared to put in at least 50 per cent more effort than you did in the last ten weeks of your previous role. You need to do your research in terms of what the role entails and what some of the potential problems are likely to be. Develop a personal to-do list of things to prepare or put in place. Think also about how you will need to change. How will you behave differently, what knowledge will you need to gain and what new skills would be useful? Understanding these things will help to build your confidence.

Learn as much as you can about the company and the department you will be working in, the company's strategy, its customers and suppliers. Think about the perceptions that people have and, of course, what the structures are that you will have to work with.

There are a number of ways in which to do this:

→ use your network;

→ research the company website;

→ talk to your new boss;

→ read the trade press;

→ trawl the internet for stories and articles;

→ read the annual reports – your company's and particularly those of your major customers.

QUICK TIP **PREPARE AHEAD**
Research is never wasted. Keep good notes of what you
have found out and ensure that they are easy to access –
you will be surprised what will become useful at some point.

There will be times in the next ten weeks when you will feel overwhelmed, so prepare for it. For instance, set up a way to capture key
things you have learnt each day, create a to-do list and ensure that you
store ideas on how to change things. Capture items that you may want
to build into your vision document and two-year strategy.

Most importantly, be prepared to hit the ground running: you don't
want to spend the first ten weeks playing catch-up.

What do the first ten weeks look like?

Use the following suggestions to put together a plan for the first ten
weeks in your new position.

Week 1: Get to know your stakeholders
First impressions will influence the way relationships develop. Start by
understanding the key internal stakeholders, what their roles are and
how each could impact on your success. These will include the people
who report to you, your boss and certainly the sales director. You may
come into contact with other directors, and you need a good contact
into finance, probably through your financial controller. Then there's marketing and others appropriate to your situation.

Assess each stakeholder group on a power versus support matrix
(see figure overleaf). Focus on those stakeholders who have the greatest power or influence over your effectiveness. Plan how you can win
round those that may be working against you, and consider ways of
using the support of your advocates. This way you can make sure that
internal politics operate in your favour. Influence does not always go with
position. Take the example of a sales team with an old retainer who has
been in the team since time began. He has seen off a number of upstart
new managers and he's prepared to see you off too. There is a good
chance that he thinks that the way the team has done things for the last

ten years is still just right. It is likely that you and your boss think that change is needed.

This person will have high influence over the team unless you use the weight of your boss to help at least to make the old salesman pipe down a bit, and you need to talk to the rest of the team to make sure that they buy into what you are saying. Probably the best you can hope for is to get such a person into the resister/low influence part of the matrix below, unless he really is damaging things, in which case use the first ten weeks to think about how to move him on to other pastures.

So, it's not just where the stakeholders are now that you are considering but where you want them to be.

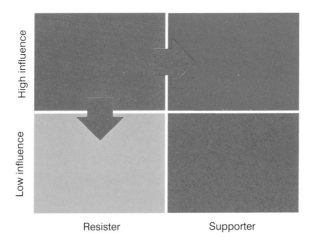

Assess the situation quickly. Make a good impression and be positive: don't make it look like everything you have taken over is wrong. Try not to be a 'know it all'; in fact just be yourself without actually trying to impress. You're good, so a good first impression will happen naturally. I have seen many managers who come into an organisation shouting, 'Look at me, look how good I am, look what I know about you'. This doesn't impress; in fact it has just the opposite effect. You don't need to be doing or saying anything profound at this stage – management have hired you because they think you are the best person for the job. Mind you, don't let them think they have made a mistake. You need to have done the research on the organisation, but use that knowledge to ask good questions and build on this knowledge; don't use it to show off.

Prepare carefully for meetings and plan your behaviour too. What is the impression you want to give and what do you need to do to make sure this will happen? Be aware that people will be looking at you asking themselves, 'Why are they so special?' 'What ideas do they have?' 'What will they want to change?' They are also watching for you to slip up, or waiting for you to give something away about yourself. This, I'm afraid, is particularly true of salespeople; they like to know what they might get away with. You have a significant advantage in the first few weeks – you don't have to prove yourself. Use it wisely and just be careful not to make a stupid mistake.

Be objective. Do not assume. Don't get caught up in the detail, keep the big picture in view the whole time. Don't take sides or be influenced by the strongest characters: they are not always the best ones to be guiding you. You don't need to prove anything yet. If you don't know, say that you don't know. This makes sure your lack of knowledge doesn't count against you. You have the luxury right now not to know, you can use that to your advantage. Listen, seek to understand and don't go on about what it was like in other companies.

On the other hand, don't just do what you are comfortable with – be prepared to stretch yourself. Build momentum, trust and credibility. Promote yourself, but do not boast. Identify sponsors and watch out for those who express only negative views and are prepared to stab others in the back during their chats at the coffee machine. I quite like the term 'well poisoners' to describe such people. Praise good work from your team, and take responsibility, for good and bad, being careful not to shift blame.

Try to find out what your predecessor did, and what worked well and what didn't work so well. How does the vital system of communication work in the company and what gets in its way? I have seen a new manager take over from someone who failed to reach their target and assume that everything that their predecessor did was wrong. In fact only about 5 per cent was wrong, and could have easily been fixed by putting some simple procedures in place, just to get the team on track. Instead he went about changing everything, including some of the team. He became totally overwhelmed, the team ended up confused and demotivated and he lasted less than six months.

Hold one-to-one meetings with all those who report directly to you in order to ask these types of questions:

→ What are the main challenges in your job?

→ What do you enjoy most?

→ What is less appealing?

→ What training have you had in the past?

→ What help and support will you want from me?

Set up weekly team meetings (and ensure the team enter the dates and times in their diaries) that reveal the activities that have gone on in the past. Get to know the team's personal and business objectives and how well they've achieved them in the past.

Try to find out all you can about your boss. What are their priorities and their experience? Find out what they expect from you and how they will measure your performance. Ask and observe how they go about their role as a manager. They have strengths and weaknesses, likes and dislikes: the more you know about them, the more effective you will be.

QUICK TIP *KNOW YOUR BOSS'S BOSS*

Try to find out about your boss's boss as well; after all, they will be involved when the time for your next promotion comes up.

At the end of the week analyse what you have learnt and create a short- and medium-term outline of a plan. Communicate and discuss ideas with your boss, but don't necessarily look to make any changes at this stage. It's good to try to identify some 'quick wins' that you could deliver in week 4. This is quite difficult but if something obvious pops up, just do it now – geniuses make their own rules.

Here's a brilliant example of making a great splash early on in a new outfit. A manager I know moved from one telecommunications company to another that was much larger and longer established. He knew, from his competitive knowledge and from things said at the interview, that senior management were implementing a huge change programme aimed at knocking the old-fashioned corners off those managers who had served with the organisation since time immemorial.

Many of these people were accustomed to a hierarchical, rather deferential, culture where seniority counted highly. They were also struggling with the concept that the customer was king. On his very first day the new boy took action on this, using the car park as his vehicle, if you'll pardon the pun. He removed every car parking space allocated on the basis of management seniority. He reallocated the best spaces to customers only. Also in his tour of the car park, he realised that there were some areas that were not only dark but also outside the range of the security cameras. Accordingly, he allocated the next best spaces nearest to the entrance to those women who sometimes or regularly worked late. At a stroke he got the support of those of his people who felt held back by the old guard and of the more ambitious women willing to work long hours. His action also became high profile without his having to tell a soul – the old guard did it for him – they were in an absolute furore. They sent angry emails to human resources and senior managers in all parts of the organisation complaining about this stripping of their hard-earned privilege. They themselves gave him the oxygen of publicity. By the end of literally his first day his name was very high profile; he had sorted out the resisters from the enthusiasts to change, and impressed on senior management his grasp of what they were looking for in terms of cultural change. Senior management congratulated themselves, modestly of course, for hiring the right person for the job.

Week 2: Capture a business snapshot of your customers and your company

Now examine the marketplace in which you are operating, starting with existing **customers**. Find out, for example, who the most profitable are. Remembering that in most cases 80 per cent of profits come from the top 20 per cent of customers, get round the biggies as fast as you can – at least three during this week. Make sure that by the end of the meeting you have discovered the following:

→ their perception of your company

→ their characteristics and what they have in common with your company;

→ why they do business with your company;

→ what their priorities, main profit drivers and critical success factors are this current year;

→ even if only from their annual report, something about their long-term strategy.

Find out the key account strategy in your company and how the treatment of key accounts differs from the others. Note the criteria used to select key accounts and put it on your action list to review these. Frequently key accounts lists miss out major opportunities simply because a key player in the market you are selling to doesn't do any business with you at the moment.

Complete your market research by meeting with the marketing department and talking to everyone – customers, your team and your boss.

Turning then to your own **company**, before you meet with your team to analyse the current situation, do some background preparation. You need to know the following:

→ the company's soft data: its history, mission, values, vision and strategy;

→ the unique selling points that differentiate its products and services;

→ the culture and its associated strengths and weaknesses.

Find out how good your company is at making changes by discussing a major change with someone who was involved. You need to know who the movers and shakers were because they will probably be your change agents in the future. Look for the skeletons in the cupboards that you're going to have to sort out. These can be anything from festering customer satisfaction issues to log-jammed administration involving unpaid and disputed invoices.

Now turn to the future and the following hard data:

→ the sales processes that are in place, including how sales people plan sales campaigns and the customer relationship management system, however formal or informal it might be;

→ sales tools and pipeline management measurements;

→ key performance indicators (kpis), budgets and targets;

→ how the team capture and communicate best practice – if someone has made a good win, is there a medium for them to communicate this to their colleagues, and likewise for mistakes and losses?

By this time you should have formed a view of why things are done the way they are. It could be just 'the way they have always been done' or a system that has been carefully thought through and developed over time. You will have read a mass of internal documents, internal newsletters, whitepapers, financial reports, brochures and marketing literature, and looked at the company's website and the intranet. Just as you met with marketing to understand the soft data, meet with the finance people to get confirmation of the hard data.

While you are by no means making decisions at this time, you will have formed some views on, for example, how you can use the strengths of the organisation to increase sales. You know the weaknesses as well and have some options in mind for dealing with them. Always spend more time focusing on the strengths, but be prepared to help your team put the weaknesses into perspective. They're sales people after all, so they tend to blame lack of performance on areas outside their control – whilst their positive results are usually down to what they do and how they do it whatever the odds.

At the end of the week analyse what you have learnt and create a short- and medium-term action plan. Communicate and discuss ideas with your boss, but don't look to make any changes at this stage. However, try to identify some quick wins that you could deliver in week 4.

Week 3: Create a team SWOT

Right, time to get to know your team. Create criteria for evaluating your team and identify those areas that you consider to be strengths and weaknesses, their activities, what they do, their knowledge, skills and aptitude.

Get to understand your team, the overperformers and underperformers, and how their results have developed over the past three years. Look at past appraisals to gauge their knowledge and skills and where they need help and support. Work out what development approach has worked for them in the past – coaching, training, motivating, directing or mentoring. Ask them about their motivation, what turns them on and off. Look at the team dynamics – how the team works, who is dominant, who has the best ideas and how they all relate to each other.

Recognise what they have done well and the success they have had, and let them know what you have noticed by discussing the specifics – not generalities. It's important that they sense that your first impression of them is positive. Summarise your thoughts in the form of a SWOT analysis – in terms of meeting or achieving its objectives, what are the team's strengths, weaknesses, opportunities and threats?

Recognise that this will reflect your first impressions, so some of your conclusions will be valid whilst others may be incorrect. Take time to validate your thoughts with your boss and other key stakeholders – this will provide an opportunity to get to know the team better and to start thinking about ways to address weaknesses and exploit strengths. Here's an example:

Strengths	Weaknesses
Highly motivated team with good range of experience The recent launch of a new product range with several unique selling points	Poor communication and cooperation between sales and other departments No sales processes in place, leading to inconsistent dealings with customers and prospects and probably loss of sales
Opportunities	Threats
Customers demanding greener solutions creates opportunities for cross selling Can use existing products and services in other new segments with no additional costs	Competition from developing countries with cheaper and less sophisticated products and services Customers and prospects in existing sectors starting to merge

This manager has identified weaknesses in the way that the departments work together and that there are no formal sales processes in place. At the same time, they believe that they have a great team and the company has some exciting products and services to sell to existing and new customers. If you were them, what actions would you consider?

At the end of each week analyse what you have learnt and create a short- and medium-term plan about the development of the team. Communicate and discuss ideas with your boss. Don't look to make any changes at this stage, but try to identify some quick wins that you could deliver in week 4.

Week 4: Secure quick wins

OK, it's time to start thinking about making changes. You are aware of what needs changing and what you can leave be. You also know the changes that people have made in the past and which of them worked and which did not. Avoid reinventing the wheel; this is particularly important at this time. You're bound to have at least one old salt on the patch who has seen it all before and will be able to tell you why a new approach has already been tried, was bound to go wrong and how wrong it went. Ensure all changes you are considering have the right impact (ideally an impact on results). Analyse what skills need to be developed to implement change effectively. You need a plan for selling that to your boss so that they will agree the funds to bridge the gaps in your skills and knowledge.

Whatever decisions you take for action it is unlikely you can do it all. Set priorities based on the impact each action will have on results. You must also consider what can be done by when and the resource implications. Think about how you will measure the resources used and the benefit each initiative will deliver. You may, for example, have identified that the time the team takes to write customer proposals is lengthy and that each new proposal gains little from ones that have gone before. There could be a business benefit in using a 'proposals database', and if the salespeople see it saving time on what they dismiss as 'admin.', that's a good double whammy result. Weigh up the costs and benefits and you might have a simple but effective change to propose.

For the changes that you consider to be a priority, identify one or two that you know you can implement quickly, within a few days, and with little risk. These are referred to as 'quick wins' and will do a lot to boost your credibility within the organisation, assuming they succeed. You can ensure success by thinking carefully about what could be the potential problems, and taking time to meet with the relevant stakeholders to understand what needs to be done to mitigate them. Decide on the best way to communicate these quick wins in a way that builds commitment from your team and the stakeholders. Make sure you credit the team, not yourself. It's time enough to claim the credit during your appraisal.

At this stage an effective quick win needs to be low risk but have the potential to improve results. Make sure it is aligned with the company strategy, although it may not be in an obvious area of people or customer management. Think about holding a one-day workshop to generate ideas on:

→ the introduction of new systems;

→ sales tools and measures;

→ agreeing 'SMART' objectives (specific, measurable, agreed, realistic and time bound);

→ training;

→ internal and external meeting formats and agendas;

→ changing or increasing levels of responsibility;

→ restructuring;

→ prospect and key account selection criteria;

→ communication across departments.

It would be sensible to ask each team member to do some work before the workshop and get them to present their ideas to the whole team. You could act more as a facilitator. In this way you will build credibility and start to resolve some of the issues directly affecting your company's results. It's an important time to build consensus, but take care not to be seen as a ditherer – in the end a number of these matters are your decision. Run one-to-one meetings with your team. Get them involved in how you are going to run things. Give them feedback and encourage them to give their feedback on you and what you are doing. Don't promise the moon: it's likely that the result of your changes will not materialise for three to six months, so ensure you have the right expectations.

QUICK TIP UNDER-PROMISE AND OVERPERFORM
Managers love nice surprises but hate nasty ones.

Week 5: Create a vision

You have now successfully completed your first month and have made an excellent impression on all the stakeholders. You have learnt a significant amount and gathered invaluable insight and information. It is now time to plan how you will use this longer term. Where do you want your team to be in two years? Think specifically about your vision, what you think a good outcome will look like at the end of the period. Draft the goals you need to set and how you will help your team to achieve them.

Your vision should also clearly articulate your approach to each of the Fast Track top ten processes, as well as what you see as the biggest gaps and how and when each will be closed. At this stage the vision does not need to be detailed, but it should provide a roadmap stating clearly what you are looking to achieve.

Talk it through with your team, then with your boss, or if there's a lot of controversial change with your boss first. Your vision may include selling to a customer sector that hasn't been tapped before. Perhaps with only a few hours of sales training you could increase your sales by a significant percentage over time by offering the same product or service to a completely new set of customers. Recently, a company significantly increased sales by offering exactly the same components it sells to white goods' producers to producers of wind turbine equipment.

Finally, at this stage you should reflect on your new role and ensure that you are able to achieve everything you set out to do without destroying the balance of work commitments to your preferred lifestyle. You may have to work a bit harder and longer at this time, but the aim is to get it down to a sensible day's work as quickly as possible.

Week 6: Take a break!

OK it's the end of week 5 and you've done a great job, but it is likely to have sapped a significant amount of energy. No matter how energetic you are as a new manager, you need to slow down for a while. Use this week to take time to relax and get to know the team better. Spend more time with each of them on a one-on-one basis and listen to their views, their aspirations and their concerns. You need to know the whole person, so discuss their activities outside work as well as the job. Talk to your key stakeholders and test the various elements of your vision, updating it as you go.

Pay particular attention to your boss and continue to get to understand them better. By now you should have a good idea of their preferred leadership style, so think about how you can operate most effectively with that style. Ask them how they feel your first five weeks have progressed.

During this week make sure you get on top of your day-to-day administration and clear as much of your in-box as possible. Take time to delegate non-critical tasks to members of the team as early as possible. Remember that it is much better to deal with issues early, before they become crises. Look at some recurring problems: is there anything you can do to stop them recurring, instead of just using sticking plasters?

Week 7: Build your reputation

Recognise that your new role is fundamentally different from your previous role and that in order to succeed you may need to do things differently. This is particularly important when it is your first role in management, where you will have switched from achieving results through your own efforts and expertise to achieving results through others. In many cases you have been promoted because you were good at delivering results for yourself; the skills required to do this through other people are very different. Recognise that your personal reputation will now be dependent on the ability of the team to deliver results. Most sales managers were pretty good salespeople beforehand and it's probably more difficult in this role than others to let the team get on with it without interfering. If you interfere all the time you will build a culture of dependency and stifle their creativity and energy.

Think about the different meetings (internal and external) you attend on a week-to-week basis and how you should behave on each occasion. What has worked in the past that you can use in the future?

Take time to build your network. The more senior you become, the more important your network will be to your future success. Be critical in terms of how you use your time, as some of the network organisations you can join in person or on the internet promise a lot but deliver little. Seek to identify and bring in best practices from other organisations. You'll find that there are particular areas where people continually say that they don't have the information they need and others where they complain about information overload. Think about addressing that.

Week 8: Analyse your team's pipeline

Your quick wins will have given you a feel for what is possible, but more importantly they will have helped to build your reputation as someone who gets things done. You will have established relationships with key people across the business. Your team will want to be moving forward with you, so now is the right time to give them the responsibility to improve the business results.

A good place to start is to analyse the team's pipeline, their list of active prospects and sales projects. Find the answers to these questions:

→ What is the team's total target in terms of sales revenue and profitability?

→ What are their individual targets?

→ What is the average spend and profitability likely to be for buying customers?

→ What can they do to increase the average spend of customers?

→ How many buying customers do they need to achieve their target?

→ What is the typical conversion ratio from prospect to buying?

→ What influences conversion ratios?

→ What can they do to improve conversion ratios?

→ How many prospects do they need to work on?

→ What are the numbers looking like? How many sales calls will they have to do? Do they have time to do them all?

→ How can they improve prospect selection criteria?

End with a very clear plan, with actions and deadlines, and ensure you are in a position to monitor this regularly. Take time in one-to-one meetings to discuss performance against the plan and what corrective action may need to be taken. You know from experience that salespeople fail because they have too short a pipeline, so that at worst any single sale lost or postponed wrecks their plan. Pass that experience on.

Week 9: Reflect and learn

Now stop and review where you are. Reflect on what has gone well, what has gone badly, and why. Go back to your original plan or to-do list and check off the items you have tackled successfully, and then critically review areas where you failed to meet expectations.

Meet with your boss and ask for a formal review of your progress. Many bosses are not very good at doing formal performance reviews, but nevertheless it is an essential part of continuous improvement. Then meet with your other stakeholders and get their input into what has gone well and what they would like to see you change.

Go back to your market research and concentrate on your competitors. Who are the competitors and what makes them successful? Your knowledge of how they treat their customers, from wining and dining to providing excellent products and service, and your understanding of their strategies will show you what actions you need to take, if any.

Find out more by researching the market, meeting the marketing department, asking your customers and, possibly more importantly, asking your competitors' customers.

Week 10: Develop your two-year plan

You are now ready to embark on the next stage of your career. You have done everything required to ensure you will make a real impact on your company's future results. First of all review and update your vision. Study the successes and failures of both your company and your competitors. This allows you to develop a plan with a high likelihood of overcoming obstacles and of succeeding.

From what you have already documented by following the suggestions in weeks 1–9, you're in a position to develop a strategy. Use/consider the following:

→ the SWOT analyses you have produced;

→ your customer mix;

→ what makes your company unique – now and in the future;

→ what the trends are in the market;

→ how you are using positive trends to your advantage.

Include your team's attributes, what they do and how they do it. Your knowledge of their attributes allows you to agree development plans with them. You can keep the plan for year 2 at a high level, but plan the first three months in detail.

It may also be worth considering team structure at this stage. It may make sense to move responsibilities around, inside and outside the sales team.

Once you have your plan, identify barriers or potential problems that could get in your way. What could cause these to happen and what can you do to prevent them? Build these actions into the plan.

Finally, you should be as specific as possible about how you will know if you are succeeding. Set key performance indicators that you can monitor on a month-to-month basis that will let you and your boss know if you are on track. One good target is to increase the length and quality of the pipeline, since this recognises that normally salespeople do too little prospecting. Include other measures that are less tangible, such as strength of customer relationships, customers' perceptions of your company, and your team's individual level of knowledge in each of the key critical areas – product, processes, customer, market, competition and so on.

QUICK TIP *LOOK OUT FOR UNWANTED SIDE EFFECTS OF KEY PERFORMANCE INDICATORS*
Make sure that salespeople cannot use their personal key performance indicators in a way that makes money for them but not for the organisation.

Checklist: what do I need to know?

During your first ten weeks in a new job, start gathering information that will help you to deliver results, build your team and develop your career. Use this checklist to see if you have the necessary information – using a simple Red-Amber-Green status, where Red suggests major gaps in current knowledge and that immediate action is required, and Amber suggests some knowledge is missing and may need to be addressed at some stage in the future. Green means you are happy with your current state.

TOPIC	INFORMATION	RAG
Market	The major trends in your market, what is driving them and the opportunities and threats you can identify	
Customers	Your top customers and their specific requirements, their drivers and strategies, and why they chose to do business with you	
Suppliers	Your top ten suppliers – who they are and how they contribute to the company's results	
Business strategy	The overall strategy for the business in terms of its products and markets, and the basis on which it differentiates itself in the market	
Measurement	The key performance indicators (KPIs) that will be used to assess whether you and your team have been a success	
Stakeholders	Those individuals or groups that you will work with and that will influence success or failure	
The team	Individual members of your team – their backgrounds and experience, their knowledge, skills, motivation and aptitude, and their strengths and weaknesses	
Your boss	Your operational manager – their preferred style, what they expect from you and what it is that really makes them tick	
Resources	The people, facilities, equipment, materials and information available to you to implement your strategy	
Technology	Whether you have implemented the right technologies that improve sales effectiveness and whether they are working properly	

TOPIC	INFORMATION	RAG
Processes	Whether you have mapped the major sales processes and whether they are being followed correctly	
Scope	The boundaries that have been set for you and your team – the things you are not allowed to do	
Potential problems	The risks you face going forward – the things that could go wrong based on the assumptions you have made	
Review process	The formal review process for your internal team reviews and where KPIs will be reviewed with your boss	

STOP – THINK – ACT
Now put together your plan for your first ten weeks:

What should I do?	What do I need to achieve?
Who needs to be involve?	Who needs to be involved and why?
What resources will we require?	What information, peeple, facilities, materials or equipment will be required?
What is the timing?	When will tasks be achieved?
	Week 1
	Week 2
	Week 3
	Week 4
	Week 5
	Week 6
	Week 7
	Week 8
	Week 9
	Week 10

Visit **www.Fast-Track-Me.com** to use the Fast Track online planning tool.

EXPERT VOICE

Getting close to the customer
Professor David Birchall and Jeni Giambona

What is Intel now up to, employing anthropologists? Why have media companies commissioned observation studies of families at home? Why is Nokia supporting **shareideas.org**, an online community, and wiki for sharing ideas about how to use mobile communications for social and environmental benefits? Why does IBM run 'jamming sessions' where employees throughout the world can contribute suggestions for improvement?

This is all perhaps explained by Sir Terry Leahy, CEO of Tesco, who recently said:

> At Tesco some of our best ideas come from the shop floor, usually inspired by what our customers tell us or what our staff observe. Through simple systems and lean management structures we make sure these ideas are harvested and do not get lost in a suggestion box somewhere, which would mean we miss out on a potentially money-making idea and the person who thought of it feels ignored and undervalued. To help encourage this exchange and development of ideas we also send thousands of our head office managers out to work in store for a week every year so that they can experience the products and processes they develop and make them better, cheaper or simpler.[3]

It is clear that Tesco has been very successful in applying new information and communication technology to its business. This is particularly evident in both its Clubcard and its dotcom business. In the case of the former it has a wealth of information about its customers buying habits, which in some cases goes back to 1998. In developing its dotcom business it has made good use of technology in picking customer orders, in delivery and driver support. This has brought about considerable efficiency improvements. But Tesco emphasises the importance in the development of this business of its knowledge of its customers and their needs.

[3] Leahy, Sir Terence (2006), 'What innovation means to Tesco', *The Edge*, Swindon: ESRC UK, March, Issue 21, available at: **www.esrc.ac.uk**

These companies are all trying to get closer to customers in order to better understand what motivates them to purchase their services. In the case of Intel, it is trying to understand how communities use technology by direct observation. Similarly Nokia will get a wide range of ideas, some of which will be suitable for development into product offerings. For Tesco, it has automated the buying process in such a way that it has detailed knowledge of purchasing behaviour.

It is clear that the role of sales in this process is vital, whether the sales process is in person or it has been automated. The salesperson has direct contact with customers, has the opportunity to find out about their real needs and to then transmit this back to those who can do something about it. This sounds well and good, but I am sure that most people in direct contact with customers do not find a receptive organisation eagerly awaiting ideas and insights.

Most organisations are not achieving what Leahy hopes for at Tesco. There are many reasons for this: the 'not invented here syndrome', the resistance to something with the potential to disrupt an established way of life, the failure to recognise the potential of ideas, the lack of vision of decision makers, risk averse organisations, and so on and so forth. We can all recognise many barriers to successful implementation of new ideas. Even organisations with a well-honed new product development process do not necessarily have great success in bringing products to market.

But most innovation does come from customers placing demands on suppliers. So information is a vital first step in the innovation process.

Information, however, costs money. Much of what is collected proves of little actual use in practice. Systems are often not well designed, not only the asking of the right questions but then the means for processing the data and making sense out of it such that it is actionable. So we set out to try to develop some means by which it would be possible to assess at least the front end. How can we collect useable and meaningful data at the optimum cost?

In order to achieve this, companies have been told that being market-oriented is a 'must' if they wish to ensure their future success. But when looking to innovate just how much does the customer's view really matter? Moreover, in what ways can the customer really be involved? There seems to be confusion in what has been published as to the appropriate role of customer input. Hence, one of the questions facing firms is that of how to involve customers in an effective manner in order to make sure that innovations meet what the market (customer) requires.

Of course, there are many forms of customer involvement: focus groups, questionnaires, interviews, feedback forms and all the information collected by the customer service department. If it is to serve the purpose of meeting

EXPERT VOICE

customers' needs in developing new products, all this information must be interpreted and shared across those parts of the firm directly involved in the innovation process and then embedded in appropriate ways into processes and products so as to be able to anticipate demand.

One of the most effective ways of collecting information from customers – though perhaps not the most obvious – is through their complaints, a means much used by Japanese companies but now more and more popular with European companies as well.

Listening and responding to complaints can lead to more than simply ensuring customers remain loyal. Nowadays, thanks to recent developments in technology, it is easier than ever for firms to listen to their customers' views, if they only want to, thanks to developments such as blogs and online diaries. In the US big companies have already started to make extensive use of this new way of collecting 'marketing' information by including blogs on their corporate websites. However, few British companies so far seem ready to accept this challenge. But surely soon they will recognise the full potential of this new, readily available tool.

So, let's return to ask: what do we mean by market orientation? It is really a deeply held belief in the organisation that it has to learn about the market by developing an understanding of it, and to then use the information for marketing decisions and actions. It becomes the basis of organisational behaviours with regard to the firm's business stakeholders (customers, competitors and internal functions), all of whom have an impact on organisational performance. Insights suggest that market orientation is basically a corporate culture characterised by the organisation's disposition to continuously deliver superior value to its customers. As a consequence, the market-oriented firm should have an organisation-wide commitment to continuous information gathering and coordination of customers' needs, competitors' capabilities and the provisions of other significant market agents and authorities. This results in an integrated effort on the part of the employees and across departments in organisations to better meet customers' needs.

So we set out to try to develop some means by which it would be possible to to collect useable and meaningful data at the optimum cost. In addition, we need to analyse what level of engagement may be required from stakeholders. The table opposite tries to sum up the different levels and the different possible approaches to customer involvement.

METHODS AND APPROACHES FOR STAKEHOLDERS' INVOLVEMENT

	LEVEL OF ENGAGEMENT			
Market orientation	Stakeholders given information and developments (passive)	Stakeholders are consulted	Stakeholders engage in dialogue	Management driven by stakeholders
Customer engagement approach (distributors and/or users, internal staff, suppliers)	→ Inform via public media, direct mail and other direct channels → Exhibitions → Brochures	→ Feedback sought from end users via surveys and interviews → Complaints process systematised → Returns monitored and analysed	→ Focus groups → Observation of product in use or service response → Regular measurement of perceptions	→ Long-term relationships through user groups → Direct involvement in innovation process → Concept testing
Number of stakeholder participants	Mass approach	Selected stakeholders	Limited number of stakeholders	Very limited number of regulars with direct interest in development
Applicability	→ Helps alert the market to new products and services	→ Reactive → Low cost → Normal part of good-quality processes	→ Rich information available for fundamental product/service review	→ Effective where sensitive issues arise from product use → Particular applicability in high added-value business-to-business transactions

EXPERT VOICE

LEADING THE TEAM

Even top executives need a manager; many CEOs who only have share-holders or banks to report to, seek out coaches or get guidance, support or a second opinion from peer groups. Everybody needs someone to help them gain experience and learn.

By moving to a leadership position from a sales job, you have a head start over others, simply because you already understand the complexity of dealing with people. In my experience those who struggle most with the move into leadership are those from a technical background, those who are used to dealing with machines. Although machines are often complex, they are relatively predictable; you can never say that about people, and that is what makes the job of leading people so special and, frankly, so challenging.

You will notice that I have already mixed the terms leadership and management. It is interesting that we are often called sales directors, key account managers or sales managers, but the title sales leader is still rarely used. So what is the difference between management and leadership? I like a simple definition – we manage things, processes and numbers but we lead people.

Leadership is about getting things done through others and enabling others to perform beyond their perceived limits. It sounds straightforward, but in practice it can be a tremendous challenge and quite frustrating. The temptation is often to take a shortcut and just do things yourself rather than letting the team get on with it. I have certainly seen many managers do just that. I have also met plenty of leaders who say, 'I wouldn't ask anyone to do something I couldn't do better myself'. What are your views of that approach? Think about leaders who have inspired you – from business, politics or sport perhaps – who have encouraged you to stretch yourself. What attributes do they have? Have they always been able to do everything they ask of you? If not, think about how they achieve this level of leadership and how you can develop yourself to be like them. In the end, of course, you have to be able to lead people to do things you could not even approach, let alone do better.

As a leader, although you will not be able to conduct all the tasks you ask of others, they will be looking at you for your approach to issues, your general attitude and your energy levels. Every little thing you do will be seen as a signal as to how they should behave – for instance, what time you are sending emails, what makes you laugh and what drink you order after the sales conference.

To do a sales leadership job effectively, you will need the right balance of management, looking after the processes, finance and so forth, and leadership, looking after and developing your people.

QUICK TIP BE A NET EXPORTER OF TALENT
People like joining teams where they know there is a good chance of getting promoted out of it.

Changing myself

How should I think?

Moving upwards in an organisation requires considerable change. Just because you excelled in your previous role doesn't guarantee success in your new one. Transferring from being a member of a team to a leader of a team can demand tremendous adjustments, especially if you were competing against other team members when selected for the job. For the first time in your career there may also be a significant sense of loneliness that will be different from anything you have experienced before. You will be expected to take responsibility, not only for your own actions but also for those of others. You will be delegating tasks you were used to doing yourself and will have to accept responsibility when things go wrong, even though you were not the person who made the error.

It is very useful to have gathered leadership experience outside work (you should encourage your team to do this). You will be able to refer to this experience in your role as a sales leader. The fundamentals are very similar; don't ignore everything you have learnt just because it wasn't in a work environment.

To lead a team, you first need to know yourself, understand what influence you have over others and where you strengths and weaknesses lie. Your team will now be looking to you for an example. Little things you say, even as throwaway comments, little things you do or the way you respond to situations will have an influence on how your team see you and how they interpret the direction you want them to go in.

You will probably have to change your behaviour more than you were expecting. The way you think as a leader will be very different; you will need to look at things from a higher level. The term 'helicopter view' is very relevant here – you are used to seeing things from 'ground level', now you will need more of an overview. You need, for example, a better understanding of company strategy and how sales contributes to it. You will have to make bigger, further-reaching decisions and look further into the future than you have been used to.

 CASE STORY *CONTAINER SHIPPING COMPANY, MIKE'S STORY*

Narrator Mike was responsible for all export sales and marketing in the UK for a container shipping company. UK exports were struggling to compete, so he was tasked with coming up with innovative approaches to boost sales effectiveness.

Context The firm was one of the world's leading container shipping companies, offering its customers top quality, door-to-door solutions and a comprehensive global coverage.

Issue Mike was aware that salespeople were not selling effectively to different customer segments. They did not have the necessary knowledge of the industry that the customer was in. This also meant that customers were not always getting the optimum level of support from the sales team.

Solution Mike restructured the sales team and aligned the structure to the customer characteristics. Each team handled at best one, at most three, different types of customer.

Learning Ensure that the sales team structure is aligned to the customer characteristics and not based on what is right for you. This will mean segmenting your customers effectively and may require having to improve some of your salespeople's knowledge and skills. In the end you may have to change some salespeople.

What personal attributes will I need?

First of all, do not abandon the attributes you developed and used as a salesperson – energy, resilience, confidence and so on. All these will still be required, but there are three attributes that you will urgently need to develop further when you are in the leader's chair – coaching skills, skills in making business cases and skills in developing your team.

Coaching skills

The first element of good coaching is good listening. Good listeners make good salespeople; so you already have good experience of listening to customers and not only hearing what they say about their problems and opportunities but also hearing what they mean and how they feel about you, your company and the solutions that you are proposing. But the leader has to take listening to a new level.

Think of it like this. When a salesperson comes to you of their own volition they probably arrive with a problem – business or personal. Often you will recognise the problem, having dealt with similar ones in the past, and be able to give some quick suggestions as to what they might do. You may be right, but what you are doing is not necessarily constructive. If you give salespeople instant solutions to their problems they will come to depend on you and fail to develop.

This is where coaching skills come in. You listen to the problem and then ask questions about possible solutions. Then you listen to them while they work out what they should do, thinking aloud as it were. Your aim is to prompt them to come up with a solution themselves. It may not be as good as yours but it belongs to them and they will be committed to it. It also means that they are developing their problem-solving skills. The ultimate you are aiming for, is for them to come to you not with problems but with potential solutions and preferably a recommendation as to what should be done. That way you will improve performance and make the best use of your time.

Skills in making business cases

The next main reason why your people will come to you is to ask for resources. They want demo facilities, support staff, travel expenses, permission to entertain clients and so on. Again you could just make a decision, considering whether your budget can afford what they are asking. Or, much better, you can ask them to justify the expense in terms of sales or profit. Encourage them to do a cost/benefit exercise on all major requests for resources. In order to be able to do this properly you yourself need to be familiar with the terms of investment appraisal – cost justification, payback method, discounted cash flows and so on. If these are a mystery to you, find some training or use a book to learn. After all, your next step is second line management and you will at that level be expected to run a profit and loss account and justify your budget or variations to it. You will also need to make business cases for capital investment.

If your sales team are good at developing business cases they are much more likely to be able to explain the return on investment a customer will get if they buy the proposed solution.

Skills in developing the team

There is no doubt that the best managers are net exporters of talent. They develop their people to such an extent that other managers will pilfer them and their boss's boss will promote them. This is a great attribute since it means that you will get a reputation not only for being good with your own career but also for being someone who expects people to arrive in the team, learn and grow. This makes your team an attractive one for the best people to join, and that's what you want.

This can be a formal or an informal process but I recommend that you formalise it. This means that in addition to their annual appraisal, each member of the team will also have a personal development plan showing the training they should go on in the next 12 months and the job experience they need to be able to grow.

Work on these three areas and you will make a quick and effective changeover to the new leadership role.

What leadership style is appropriate?

Do you tell 'em or sell 'em? Some people talk about 'push and pull' management styles. Push is the 'Do what you are told' or autocratic method; pull is the consulting, democratic way of leading people. You need a combination of the two for different people and different situations.

You will find that your natural style will work very effectively with some members of your team, but probably not all. To understand how you need to adjust your preferred style for each individual reporting to you, you will need to really, and I mean *really*, understand them. Use previous assessments of your team made by others as a guide, but use your own skills in getting to see how they react and perform in as many situations as possible, both in and outside work.

It is also essential to adapt your style according to the experience of each team member. Those new to sales will probably be very enthusiastic, willing to please and go the extra mile, but they may need more direction, push, from you. Those who have been in the job two to four years may become despondent, not realising that they have actually come a long way. This is because they are only focused on the mountain they still have to climb, realising just how complex the job is and the knowledge and skills they still need to develop. They could be frustrated if their results are poor or dropping just at the time when they expect them to be improving. They will need a lot of encouragement: a coaching style is more appropriate, reinforcing the fact that they can do it themselves, giving them confidence and improving their motivation.

QUICK TIP *BE EXTRAVAGANT WITH PRAISE WHERE APPROPRIATE*
Some people need constant reassurance that you are pleased with what they are doing. Identify them and give them what they need.

When salespeople have been in the job for ten years or more, they are going to work fairly autonomously, but they will probably not like it if you put all your time and effort into the other members of the team. However, directing and coaching them can appear patronising, so what do you do? Firstly, you must definitely spend as much time with them as with the others. Help them to take more responsibility and behave even more autonomously. Involve them in strategic planning, high-level decision making, new product or service launches or expanding the customer base. If such team members want to move up the organisation, your responsibility is to help develop their skills to enable them to do so. If they don't, and that is often the case, ensure that their aspirations are understood and are being met. Perhaps there are additional responsibilities they would like, such as mentoring some of the more junior members of the team or taking over some of the strategic key accounts.

You will need to think when it is more appropriate to address topics in a one-to-one meeting and when they would be better handled in team meetings or informal 'get togethers'. Also consider how to structure your meetings. All team meetings will need to be formal, with agendas (published in advance) and action points. Consider running team meetings once a week, starting with you covering performance figures, then giving each salesperson 10 minutes to cover a topic of their choice and then you wrapping up the meeting with clear next steps. Normally it is impossible to get salespeople to stop talking in meetings; however, occasionally even salespeople can find it difficult to speak up, so then your listening skills will have to be at their best. Encourage your team, even help them, to develop their assertiveness.

No matter what leadership style you have or need for your individual team members, it is essential that you are consistent in everything you do: the way you run meetings, how you coach, your humour, the way you recognise good work and so on.

Motivating the individual

How do I get the most out of each member of my sales team?

Reward success. We tend to think of rewards as being money, but there are many other effective ways to reward your people. Sometimes just a 'Well done' can be the biggest motivator – many of us respond to recognition, so long as it is not overused. Refer to something specific and show that it is genuine appreciation. You cannot overestimate the impact this has: a phone call from you, a letter from the CEO, passing on an email from a customer and so on. Many times people take such things home to show their spouse, partner or even children. If it is a letter or email, put a copy on their personnel file. Other no-cost ideas could include presenting to a team meeting or knocking off early on a Friday. Some low-cost ideas could be small gifts for their kids, car wash tokens and theatre or cinema tickets. How about buying them a good book on effective sales? For special rewards, there is always the long weekend away or a week's sports car rental, a series of spa treatments, golf lessons or a balloon trip. If you are going for the expensive option, think carefully, because high-value rewards can end up becoming the norm and then when results take a dive or a new CFO comes in they are abandoned. The impact of dropping incentives can be more demotivating than the original idea was motivating.

Do be careful to match the reward to the person. I was with a sales team recently who were complaining about getting vouchers to take their partners out for dinner. Many didn't have partners, or were out for dinner so much with work that it wasn't a treat.

Always look for opportunities to give positive feedback; it is best to do this for individual excellence. You can recognise and reward a team, but often this has a smaller impact than an individual pat on the back.

Create the right environment

Why is this important?

The morale of a sales team is very significant. Customers can smell fear and desperation; so no matter how tough things are it is very important to have a selling environment that people can feel proud of and look forward to coming into in the morning. There's a balance here though. Selling happens when salespeople are out of the office talking to customers. So you don't want the atmosphere in the to be office to be so conducive that people much prefer to be there than out in the world of buying and selling. I think hot-desking helps in this area. Each sales person has a cupboard and drawer to keep their stuff, but they have communal use of desks. You can still have a great atmosphere, but it's not the team's second home.

The key word to describe the environment is 'professional'. Professionalism sells. Customers like to buy from salespeople who treat them professionally, do things on time and present an excellent image of their company. So, hot-desk or not, get everyone to tidy up their desks and cupboards whenever they leave the office. Make sure the decoration is smart, the office is cleaned and that the whole support mechanism behind the salespeople, from the person answering the telephone to the security person at the door to all the other professionals involved, present the same image – professional and dependable.

QUICK TIP **DON'T GIVE THEM SOMEONE TO BLAME**
When salespeople miss out on an order they look for some aspect of the company that they do not control to blame, so avoid this by making all behaviour professional.

Success breeds success and nowhere is this truer than in a sales office. A successful team measures itself by sales made, and when things are going well in this area there is a spring in the step of the whole team. The only downside of this is arrogance. Watch out for it and nip it in the bud. What you are looking for is self-confidence well short of swagger.

When times are tough it's more difficult to keep up morale. The best tip for handling hard times is to tell the truth and keep the team abreast of what is happening. Hold a planning meeting that starts with an admission that things are tough, and then ask the meeting for ideas on how to make more sales, find more prospects and keep costs down to a minimum. You may be surprised by what they come up with.

What culture is best?

The culture in a company can exist at a number of levels.

Corporate culture is developed over years; it is partly set by the senior leaders through their own leadership style. It is often summarised in vision, mission and value statements. However, there can often be a mismatch between what culture senior leaders want and what actually develops. The employees also set corporate culture by the way they respond to senior managers, directives and, of course, customers.

Leaders influence the corporate culture through:

→ their own behaviours and actions – the team will follow your lead;

→ the type of staff they hire and promote – you don't tend to hire people whose view on culture you find suspect;

→ the way employees are rewarded – this really affects behaviour you want to encourage or suppress;

→ the working environment – make it very professional.

Subcultures can also coexist at departmental or section levels. These are influenced by the departmental leaders and, in some cases, dominant employees in exactly the same ways that leaders at corporate level influence corporate culture.

Typical cultures that exist include the following:

→ **Caring or blaming.** Caring is much better; a rule by terror rarely lasts.

→ **Team or independent.** Form people into a team when you can; the total is much more than the sum of the parts. On the other hand, there are people, particularly I find in sales teams, who are loners and work better by themselves. Respect that choice.

→ **Taking responsibility or not taking responsibility.** In the long run giving people more responsibility makes them bloom and grow.

→ **Learning or closed.** Always emphasise the need for everyone to learn.

→ **Fun or serious.** People who enjoy their work achieve more.

→ **Open or not open to change.** Try hard to stay flexible.

→ **Clock watching, flexible working or long working days.** Make it horses for courses if you can, so each person chooses their own hours of work, if that does not impede customer service.

→ **Conservative or radical.** Go for it – higher-risk strategies tend to have higher returns.

Measure it – ask colleagues to describe the culture. Perhaps you should conduct surveys to establish where it is now and how it changes over time. This can also help to identify the difference between the desired and the actual culture.

Building the team

What makes a great team?

It is rare that strong year-on-year results will come from a team where there are one or two superstars. In your annual plan, take this into account as you assign roles and responsibilities.

Ideally you need a good balance of character types that complement each other. Dr Meredith Belbin did significant work on how to classify team members and then how to construct the right balance for an effective team. Belbin devised nine natural 'team roles' that each of us would tend towards in certain situations:

→ the implementer

→ the plant

→ the resource investigator

→ the coordinator

→ the shaper

→ the monitor evaluator

→ the team worker

→ the completer-finisher

→ the specialist.

Belbin concluded that the combinations of team roles could have a significant impact on the effectiveness of a team and building a team, with a balance of roles improving its effectiveness. In practice, teams cannot always contain the ideal mix, due to size or being made up of existing team members. If this is the case, it is important that members of an existing team recognise their own role under one of these headings and learn to use it, accept it and make it fit in with the other members of the team. It is also possible for individuals to play different roles once they are aware of what is needed. Some people seem to have an instinctive sense of what is missing in their team and have the capacity and the flexibility to play a different role from their natural one.

The most successful teams are made up of:

➔ the right leader;

➔ one strong plant;

➔ a spread of mental abilities;

➔ an overlap in team role capacities;

➔ jobs that fit the member's attributes;

➔ an ability to adjust to an imbalance in the team.[1]

Here is a checklist of the attributes of a great team. Which of these are present in your set-up and which need work?

➔ The team has great clarity in its goals and a sense of purpose.

➔ You as the leader are an enthusiastic supporter of your team taking responsibility for its results.

➔ The team accepts that things will change; you need to change just to keep achieving the same results.

➔ The team has shared values and a common set of operating principles – they are dedicated to making sales but in a way that is consistent with the culture of the team and the organisation.

➔ The team has a general respect for each other.

➔ The team will be very open and honest in their communication with each other.

➔ The team takes time out to develop and learn from each other and outside sources.

[1] For more about team roles, see **www.belbin.com**

QUICK TIP **SPOT THE NEXT LEADER**
When someone looks as though they will become a leader,
give them extra responsibilities and tell the team that you
are doing it.

How do I handle difficult people?

Some people in your team may be difficult to deal with. They may be aggressive, disruptive, negative or closed to new ideas. Check first to see whether it is just with you that they are like this. If that is the case, it could be your management style that needs addressing. It is possible that they feel they should be in your job, or that you are not qualified to do it. If they respond better to others than to you, what is different about the approach of those they respond well to?

If they behave in the same way with everyone, why do you think they do it? Try to put yourself in their shoes. Even though you may have completely different characteristics, you may be able to spot why they behave that way. It could be because they want to be recognised; perhaps they are insecure; or maybe they think they are capable of doing more than you are giving them. Occasionally they may think they are better than they really are.

How do you naturally react to them when they are being difficult? You can try to ignore their behaviour, or get aggressive or defensive. Check what is the right response. Look for what you can do to improve your response. Understand and control your emotions and recognise emotions in others.

Ultimately you want them to change their behaviour, so you need to find out why they are acting that way and what you need to do to get them to change. If they are looking for recognition or more responsibility, this can be relatively easy to address. If they want more responsibility but are not capable, how can you help them reach the level they aspire to? Maybe they need your help or external help, or perhaps they just need to be aware of where they need to improve. It is more effective if they can discover this themselves, so you may want to put them in a low-risk situation where they get to discover their own shortcomings.

Salespeople who have achieved their targets regularly can be particularly difficult. They feel invincible and that they can do what they like. You have two choices here. Either take them aside and explain why their behaviour is damaging the rest of the team and therefore the overall team result, or try giving them more responsibility. If this does not work, consider getting rid of them. They are indeed the bad apple that can rot the barrel and you may have to take action to protect the rest of the team and stop the team becoming frustrated or demotivated.

How should I develop the team?

Often you do not have the choice over your team members, so you will need to develop them to become an effective unit. Once again, knowing your people is paramount. Ideally you will have a good balance of people types; however, as they are all in sales, you may find some essential character types are missing. You will need to consider how to compensate for this, maybe bringing people in from other divisions for certain tasks or developing people who show some of those tendencies. With a team of salespeople they are likely to thrive in a fast-paced environment with plenty of competition and challenge.

Allow team members to develop themselves. Have a vision and a strategy that is easy for everyone to understand; then give your team members the responsibility of implementing it.

→ **Set objectives.** What is required to achieve the desired results? This could be the number of customer meetings, but it could also be to improve questioning skills, know more about the new product or service, or handle objections better.

→ **Monitor.** Track what team members are doing and the results of what they are doing.

→ **Analyse.** Really understand what they are doing and the results of what they are doing. This will also require a financial understanding that you may not have needed in previous roles. You may now have to read a balance sheet in order to understand your profit and loss account.

→ **Plan.** Agree how they will change in the future and by when; also what is required to achieve that change and how you will be able to support it.

→ **Motivate.** Really understand what makes them want to do some things and not want to do others. What can you do to help them want to do things they don't want to do, but need to?

Develop the right team members. Some members of your team will come up with more helpful ideas than others – fact. Make sure you are working with them rather than with your poorer performers. It is much better to spend time with the bulk of your team and try to get their average performance up. It is, after all, the satisfactory performers who will operate well and probably come up with the best suggestions. If you spend your time training and coaching them, preparing tools to help with productivity and showing them exemplars of how to perform better, you may raise their average by a significant percentage. This improvement will be spread across more people than if you concentrate on poor performers, and your overall performance will take a big jump.

STOP – THINK – ACT

This chapter has presented ideas for managing and developing your team. The team will be key to your success as you will not be able to achieve your objectives working alone. Stop and reflect on how well you are leading the sales team and look for ways you could improve. Now think about how well the team is operating. What does each team member need from you in terms of direction, coaching or autonomy?

What should we do?	What actions do we need to take to build the team?
Who do we need to involve?	Who needs to be involved and why?
What resources will we require?	What level of investment would be required?
What is the timing?	What deadlines do we need to meet?

Visit **www.Fast-Track-Me.com** to use the Fast Track online planning tool.

Mobile sales promotions – the use of text competitions

Cigdem Gogus

Organisations constantly look for new opportunities for selling services and products. The all-pervasive nature of mobile communications has created ways of generating income not previously thought of. One such development is text competitions. But do we know enough about the development to know what their future might be and also to judge the prospects for the broader use of mobile technologies as a marketing and sales tool?

Recent research into the use of text competitions as a marketing tool on mobile phones has produced findings which reinforce what might have been expected but also introduce some challenges for practitioners entering the field. The research was based on a study of over 200 people of mixed ages who participate in text competitions from a highly regarded global organisation. The findings fall into four key areas.

Firstly, consumers are generally positive about entering text competitions and perceive several advantages/benefits of entering such competitions. They believe that it is easy, convenient and quick to enter text competitions, as well as giving them a chance to win something. They also value the immediacy of knowing the outcome. This finding indicates that companies would be better off designing campaigns which produce instant results and incorporating mechanisms that allow consumers to know immediately if they have won or not. On the other hand, perceived disadvantages only have a very small impact on consumers' attitudes. This shows that consumers are not very worried about being inundated with unwanted spam-like messages, the price of entering text competitions and possible small print regarding price information. These findings indicate that companies should continue to follow industry best practice guidelines in relation to opt-in schemes (only contacting those consumers who have given consent) and transparency with the price information as to how much it costs to enter their competitions.

The findings of this study show that these consumers perceive entering mobile sales promotions as more advantageous than disadvantageous and therefore are, in general, positive in entering such competitions. Moving forward this would suggest that companies can use mobile sales promotions as the first stage of an integrated marketing effort in building one-to-one relationships (personal and interactive brand-consumer communication) with their customers who are willing to opt in to receive marketing communications.

In this study consumers were found to have positive attitudes towards entering text competitions as long as they find the competitions useful, fun, exciting and a good use of their time. The unique features of the mobile platform, such as the interactivity, anytime, anywhere availability and context sensitivity it affords in developing marketing communications, can be used by companies to offer an array of such benefits not possible through traditional marketing channels. It is important for companies to understand the kinds of benefits consumers value, and devise their campaigns accordingly.

A very important finding points to the impact of past behaviour in determining future behaviour. Given the importance of past behaviour in determining future participation in mobile sales promotions, companies can provide more opportunities for consumers to be exposed to text competitions through various mobile marketing campaigns. An increased exposure to mobile sales promotions can encourage consumer participation, paving the way for increased popularity of such promotions and repeat participation.

Some earlier studies suggested that younger consumers are more accepting of, and more likely to engage in, mobile marketing. These studies, however, were conducted with college students and therefore tend to be biased in that direction. The findings of this study, in which the sample was recruited from a real life situation, indicate that consumers who are slightly older and have more disposable income are more interested in participating in mobile sales promotions. The results indicate that the reach of mobile marketing can be perhaps best understood by the implications (e.g. benefits and costs) of mobile marketing for different segments of consumers. In this study, a relatively older group, characterised by relatively higher disposable income, interested in having fun, excitement, spending their time well and doing something useful, had positive attitudes towards mobile sale promotions and were likely to take part in such promotions. The key is developing mobile marketing campaigns that add something of value to the brand–consumer relationship so that the consumer will be receptive to mobile marketing communications.

The research leads us to suggest that goals of sales promotions should be rethought. With the innovative uses of mobile sales promotions through new technologies (such as the online and mobile platform), there appears to be a shift from a *transactional* viewpoint of the sales promotion to a more *relational* one. This also represents a move towards a more *consumer centric* view from the *organisation centric* viewpoint. The traditional goals associated with sales promotions, which are to increase trial, price discriminate and serve as short-term tactical tools to increase sales, might not be the only goals for the new generation of innovative sales promotion initiatives. Instead the findings suggest that sales promotions may also be appropriate to deliver high customer value through higher hedonic benefits

EXPERT VOICE

(non-monetary) or improved brand–consumer relations. Focusing on these hedonic benefits as well as the utilitarian benefits of sales promotions can bring new opportunities for companies in these new contexts.

An understanding of the mechanisms that drive consumers' participation in mobile sales promotions is crucial for marketing managers when developing new services and marketing communication campaigns. The results of this study offer an important step in this direction that paves the way for future research.

GETTING TO THE TOP

Finally, think about what got you to where you are now and what you need to do to build on those efforts and attributes and continue to develop yourself. If you want to continue your advance you need to stand out amongst your peers. As you progress up the corporate ladder you need to focus continuously on performance and increasingly look up and out as opposed to in and down. Your personal network will be more and more important and you will need to start to think and act like a director.

Focus on performance

Fast Track managers know what is important and what is not. Anyone can keep busy, but those who rise to the top are those who figure out very early where to focus their activity. To do this effectively, spend time developing your key priorities and understand how they impact on your performance and the performance of your department and the organisation.

Performance snapshot: past – historic

Top leaders learn from the past. They have an ability to put a number of things together – something their child said at breakfast, a remark that a customer made at a recent meeting and an article they read that morning in the paper – and come up with an insight. You will develop that skill if you spend time thinking about and studying the past.

When instigating change or improving structures or processes, I have rarely heard a phrase uttered as often as 'Don't think you are coming up with a unique idea – we did that eight years ago and it didn't work'. As a result of this stated or implied reaction, it is very easy either to do nothing or, at the other extreme, to search for totally new initiatives. It is rare that status quo or revolutionary new approaches have the best impact on business performance.

 QUICK TIP **DON'T FORGET THE INTERNAL STRUCTURE**
When a structural change is necessary it probably involves more than one team. It is rare for a team to restructure without affecting how other people interact with them.

Because action has been taken in the past you cannot assume that the same result will occur in the future. Also just because you have come up with a completely new idea, that does not guarantee success. Therefore, I recommend that you invest time in really understanding what big initiatives were undertaken in the past and not only what the result was, but also why that result occurred. In the past perhaps the initiative was not communicated properly, or key people hadn't bought in, or the economic situation changed during the course of the change, or employees were just ready for the change and whatever the idea was it would have succeeded. Some of this will be documented, certainly the results will be, but as a leader spend the time talking to the key people about what happened and, most importantly, why the result was the way it was. Don't just look inside your own organisation or your own industry for decisions and results. You may get some clues from, for instance, politics, war and sport.

Performance snapshot: present – current situation (gap)

To come up with your key priorities and understand how they will impact on performance, it is obviously essential to understand the current situation and where the gaps are. I had a friend who would hear a strange noise in his motorbike's engine and take the whole thing apart, clean and lubricate everything, replacing any part that looked worn, then put it back together with meticulous precision. Unfortunately it then rarely worked at all and he had to take it to the garage to get it fixed. It may be improbable that something like this can happen in business, but I have seen many ambitious leaders who have done exactly the same thing because they have not been prepared to put in the work up front to understand exactly what the current situation is and identify the gaps. You may say, 'I have no time to do all that work, I am focusing on running the business'. Those I have seen rise to the top have an interesting combination of analytical skills and intuition and know very well when to use each. You will be surprised at how many very good leaders appear to be working purely on intuition but behind the scenes have invested time to gain a very good understanding of the situation and what the gaps are that need filling.

QUICK TIP *AVOID BEING PUT OFF*
If your gut instinct tells you to do something, don't let a senior person put you off without a good debate.

Performance snapshot: future – predictive

As a salesperson you will be well aware that there is a lag between your actions and results, so consider how to set your own and others' expectations. You will also know how to keep business performance on track, set milestones, ensure effective communication, understand your influence, use appropriate key performance indicators and have contingencies. It is also rare that your first idea was the right one; the successful business leaders are those who not only make decisions but are also able to modify them as they understand more about the landscape. Often the toughest decisions are those when you realise your initiative was wrong and you need a major change in direction.

In no department is it more important to get good at predicting the future than in the sales department. After all, production, financial and all other resource planning starts from the sales forecast. It really is a bit like squaring a circle. On the one hand, you want to predict huge success so that the company gears up to meet the challenge of higher sales. On the other hand, you are not going to be popular if sales do not, in the end, justify extra investment in, for example, promotions or maintenance people. The best advice is to go for it, certainly – no sales manager ever became a director by forecasting total gloom and doom – but try not to jump to forecasts until it is absolutely necessary. Forecast X for the first half year and then, when it is clear you are going to do better than that, change your prediction.

Invite challenge

Who can we get to challenge us?

Whilst operating inside your comfort zone is very pleasant, when people only work within their comfort zone the comfort zone itself starts to contract. To avoid this we need consciously to take ourselves into other ways of doing things that will feel unfamiliar to start with.

We are probably tougher on ourselves than anyone else. So challenging ourselves is a good place to start. Find regular 'quiet' time to think through what you have done right and what has not worked, and why that was. Again this will go back to understanding your own strengths and weakness; only now you will be considering how those strengths and weaknesses will impact your future roles.

As well as your knowledge, you will need to consider the skills required as you move up the organisation. These may be different from those you have excelled at in the past. You are now moving into areas such as conflict resolution, interpersonal skills and how to analyse situations and react to them. Also consider how you come across to those above you: do people see you as a leader? Do they see you as someone who has what it takes? Seek inspiration from different groups:

→ **Your own team.** What do they do that is different from your natural approach? Why is it different? How can you use some of those techniques yourself?

→ **Other internal teams.** What ideas can be shared? What common risks can be avoided?

→ **Customers.** How are their requirements changing? Think about not only what they will want in the future but also how best to sell it to them.

→ **Competitors.** What are they doing now and what are they planning for the future? If what they are doing works, don't reinvent the wheel but look at how you can take the idea and build on it.

→ **Industry advisers.** What are the experts recommending? What breakthrough tools and techniques have they developed?

QUICK TIP **BEWARE A COMPETITIVE AGENDA**
Always check who else an industry consultant is working with, and make them sign confidentiality agreements, particularly if they also work for the competition.

There is a danger that in the process of challenging yourself you realise that you need to change quite a bit, but that is unlikely to be the case; you just need to take stock of what you do well already, identify the gaps and then prioritise the actions required. Your confidence with peers and your team may be excellent, but you may feel much less comfortable in a boardroom situation. As a salesperson, you may not understand all the financial indicators and terms on the balance sheet. When developing a strategy you may have excellent experience at sales team level, but no awareness of how a merger would impact on the company, or how to go about deciding whether the company should set up offices in other countries.

What do you do about it? Get on committees at work and outside work. Get on to project teams or become a trustee of a charity. You may need to change your network and include more senior people in it. Perhaps you will have to search for a new mentor. You may need to change what you read, what you listen to (consider business podcasts instead of 1970s music). Get involved with institutes or professional bodies; write articles. Most importantly do something, don't just think about it.

How do I keep up to date?

It is very easy to rely on the information you gather in your day-to-day job. The danger of this is that it will be too narrow for you to grow into a more senior job. You will need to expand your sources of information to ensure that you are not missing ideas. This can be very time consuming, so be selective. Consider gathering information from the following sources.

→ **Trade publications, university articles, newspapers and books.** These are a great source of up-to-date thinking from a variety of experts. Talk to your contacts and read reviews to discover which publications are likely to be most useful. Be ruthless and scan for cutting-edge thinking. Be aware when they are no longer useful, either because your knowledge has improved or due to changing content when a new editor takes over.

→ **Your network.** Include your whole network – colleagues, customers, friends. Be aware of who in your network has expertise in certain areas. Try to get them to advise you of changes in thinking or new approaches they have taken.

→ **Internet.** This provides freely available information from a variety of sources, but be aware that it is typically unstructured and will contain bias. Review the websites of your 'top ten' customers and competitors twice a year and identify up to five other useful websites that provide challenging insight.

→ **Conferences, seminars and courses.** These are a valuable source of up-to-date new thinking and offer the opportunity to question ideas or discuss how they can be made relevant to your situation. Make the effort to take two or three days out of your job to attend these and then get back to the backlog of issues when you return. Before you attend, consider how you are going to record and act on the ideas that you receive. The manual the course director gives you will probably stay on your shelf, so it's important to make notes of the key points.

→ **Institutes and professional bodies.** These can offer a combination of publications, networking and conferences. Use them not just to keep up to date, but also to test ideas and theories.

Remember that institutes and professional bodies will have a far wider benefit to you on your career ladder, so don't limit the way you use them just to keeping up to date.

→ **Fast-Track-Me.com.** All the key ideas, tools and techniques contained in the Fast Track series are available via the internet at **www.Fast-Track-Me.com.** Firstly, allocate 30 minutes to visit and explore the site. It contains a rich source of tips, tools and techniques, stories, expert voices and online audits from the Fast Track series.

Try to get the balance right. I have seen many leaders who are totally up to date but are lacking in other essential elements of their role, so plan how you will keep up to date, how much time you will allocate to it, how you will record the information and how you will ensure you use it effectively.

 CASE STORY *SPECIALIST MEASUREMENT INSTRUMENTS AND CONTROLS, MEL'S STORY*

Narrator Mel set up his company in the UK 20 years ago. The company has produced a profit in every one of those 20 years.

Context The company manufactures instruments for storage and service industries involved in controlling and measuring the flow of liquids. Mel, the managing director, was thinking of retiring within five years.

Issue The next level of management was very competent and Mel had no issues with their performance in any area. However, he wasn't sure that they would have what it takes to take over the running of the company.

Solution Mel decided to hand over additional responsibilities gradually. His first step was to concentrate on giving senior managers more control of the company's profitability. He supported this by developing their knowledge and skills and implemented a structured evaluation of skills improvement.

Learning Most senior leaders are always looking for a successor. If you take the initiative to develop yourself, that will be recognised and you will get to the top much quicker.

Getting promoted

Some years ago, I was discussing with a friend whether or not I should accept an offer of promotion. His answer wasn't advice but a question: 'Which job changes have you ever regretted?' My answer was 'None'. Whenever I have asked the same question, I have got the same answer. This doesn't mean that you should accept every job offer you receive or go after every promotion, but it is helpful to look back on your career path (how it has developed, what job offers you have received, which you have accepted and why) to help you plan your future career progression.

Let's consider why people get promoted.

→ They are in the right place at the right time.

→ They are the right person for the job.

→ They are not the right fit for their existing job.

→ No one else will take it.

→ They are best person available.

→ They show leadership qualities in their existing role.

What can you do to improve your chances of promotion?

Right place, right time
Often it is possible to predict when a position will become available (in your own company or outside). Get to understand how the current incumbent operates, what people respect in them and how others would like to see the job done differently. Show your interest early and get a feel for why you may get chosen and what may stop you.

Right person for the job
Understand the job, the culture, the team you will be leading and where the role is heading. Demonstrate that you have what it takes. Make sure other people are talking well of you before you are even on the shortlist.

Not the right fit for your existing job
Although this is not a recommended route, it does happen. Often someone is put into a position for the company's convenience; they are not a

perfect fit but show potential to do well for the company. In addition to all the other advice described above, if you do find yourself as a square peg in a round hole, don't complain, but do the best you can and use it as an opportunity to move to the right job as quickly as possible, preferably a promotion.

No one else will take it

This sounds negative, but many people I know have risen to the top by doing this. One example is in a reinsurance company where a manager accepted a job running the division in the Ukraine because no one else wanted it. They excelled and within 12 months were promoted to a very senior position in head office.

Best person available

This sounds like being the right person for the job, but the difference here is that the right person for the job may not be available; they may not want it or have family commitments stopping them. So just because you are not necessarily the right person for the job, don't let that stop you going for opportunities that you want. I recently met a salesperson for a chemical company who thought he would go for an internal promotion knowing there were others far better qualified to do it. He wasn't expecting to be considered but thought it would show that he wanted to move up the organisation and give him valuable interview experience. He was astonished when he was offered the job. The two others who would have been able to do the job didn't apply because one wasn't able to move and the other was looking for a lifestyle change that this job didn't satisfy.

Show leadership qualities in your existing role

One of the biggest challenges that companies have is finding good leadership talent. When you are relatively junior in an organisation, you may not be aware that, just as in sports, there are 'scouts' constantly on the lookout for prospective leaders. They are not looking at how well you do your existing job, but whether you show the ability to do more senior leadership roles. A word of warning: don't try to show people you are someone you are not – you will eventually get found out – but always act as if you are ready to take the next step in your career.

QUICK TIP PLAY TO THE LONG TERM
When a very senior manager is talking to you, remember
that they are looking to see not just how well you are doing
this job but your potential for the future.

Becoming a director

It is a big step moving into a director's role – many say they end up
with a less interesting job as a result. Paradoxically you can end up
losing all the activities that made you join your company or industry,
and become overwhelmed with administration, meetings, legislation or
human resource issues; there is little glamour and plenty of responsibility (answering to shareholders when profits drop, making unpopular
decisions or being interviewed on television when there is a plant accident or product recall). Be aware that when you shoot for the top, the
top isn't always as it appeared from where you started. This may put
some people off, and so it should, but if you want more control, have
faith in your decision making, are able to motivate people and have a
drive to change the way a company operates, then this is where you
should be heading.

What is the role of a sales director?

A sales director will generally have the following reponsibilties.

→ Setting the overall sales strategy in line with the company's
overall strategy.

→ Communicating the strategy, the current performance against
it and expected future performance amongst sales and support people.

→ Gaining the active support of the chief executive and other
members of the board to ensure you have the right budget and
resources to achieve the strategy. I have worked with an
organisation that realised their sales team's skills were not sufficient to achieve target, but the board was not prepared to
invest in training because the existing sales revenue could not

pay for it. The sales director was unable to convince the board that an investment in the team now would generate significantly more revenue than the initial investment.

→ Ensuring members of the board are aware of customer, competitor and other external trends and the impact of each on sales performance. Then explaining the best ways to adjust the sales strategy to gain most advantage.

What will be the statutory responsibilities?

As well as heading up the sales activities throughout the business, you will have certain roles and statutory responsibilities that accompany the title of director. As a member of the board of directors, you will be involved in:

→ determining the company's strategic objectives and policies;

→ monitoring progress towards achieving the objectives and policies;

→ appointing the senior management team;

→ accounting for the company's activities to relevant parties, e.g. shareholders;

→ attending board meetings that run the company, displaying the high level of integrity that is inferred by statutory standards and the company's interpretation of corporate governance, particularly in sensitive areas such as health and safety.

You will also have to conduct yourself in a highly professional manner.

→ Directors must not put themselves in a position where the interests of the company conflict with their personal interests or their duty to a third party.

→ Directors must not make a personal profit out of their position as a director unless they are permitted to do so by the company.

→ Directors must act in good faith, doing what they consider is in the interests of the company as a whole and not for any other purpose and with no other agenda.

How do I get to the top?

First of all you have really got to want it. You will need to be very results driven and be prepared to accept that results are going to depend on the actions of members in your team. You have to know you are going to succeed, so you need to position yourself correctly.

Get noticed – demonstrate early in your career that you can do this job. Demonstrate how you act under pressure, how you delegate, motivate others, take criticism, plan and think big. Take responsibility whenever you can. Prove what you can do and, where you can't, find ways to develop the appropriate skills.

Planning your exit strategy

We have identified the reasons for getting promoted, but one very common reason for missing out on promotion is that your company cannot afford to lose you from your existing role. If they promote you, they risk losing the results you generated, plus there is a risk that you may not be able to 'step up to the plate' in the new job. It may appear to be less risky just to fill one role rather than two. Therefore, as well as proving you are the right person for the new job, you have to prove that handing over the reins to your successor is going to have no negative impact on results.

What is succession planning?

Succession planning means ensuring that you have set up your role so that it is not dependent on having you fill it. It is having built a highly skilled and motivated team, having installed the right tools and processes and having developed a successor who can build on the work you have done and not just maintain it. As I said earlier, you must spot your successor, develop their skills and gradually give them more leadership responsibility.

Handover tips

How many times have you met someone who has just been promoted but who continues to do their old job for three to six months? No matter how capable someone is, it is impossible to do both effectively. Refer back to Chapter 6 (page 122). Before they take over from you, help prepare them for their new role by giving them the information they need. Help them to build their network by personally introducing them to key people. Explain the thinking behind your strategy, initiatives and the major decisions you took; possibly set them up with a mentor. Help them identify their strengths and weaknesses and where their knowledge and skills gaps are – and then set them on their first ten weeks programme!

STOP – THINK – ACT

In this final chapter you will have identified what you need to do to get to the top in your chosen career. Stop and reflect on your career aspirations – what do you want to be doing in three years' time?

My vision	What do I want to be doing in three years' time?
My supporters	Whose support will I need to get there?
My capabilities	What capabilties and experience will I need to succeed?
My progress	What milestones will I achieve along the way?

Visit **www.Fast-Track-Me.com** to use the Fast Track online planning tool.

Twenty-first century sales management – analytical, professional, strategic

Beth Rogers

Towards the end of the twentieth century, there was a sea change in the supplier–customer interface in business markets. Distinguished sales guru Neil Rackham suggested in 1998 that in the future salespeople would have to add value in a substantial way, or purchasing managers would just lock their doors to them and sign on to an e-marketplace to post their requirement. Indeed, in a flurry of speculation during the e-boom, some commentators suggested that all salespeople would soon be redundant.

What had happened? Competition had become global. Highly qualified purchasing professionals were rationalising the number of suppliers they were prepared to work with across all their company's locations. Technology was available for reverse e-auctions, a very suitable method of buying for commodity products. It is the customer's need to source strategically that means that the sales function now has to be managed strategically. The Industrial Marketing and Purchasing Group[1] of academics did much to examine these trends and assert that a relationship between a supplier and customer needs to be viewed as an entity in its own right.

Allocating scarce resources strategically does not come easy to a profession for so long driven by the ratio of 'feet on the street' to orders taken. Since customers are very powerful, their preference has to play some part in the supplier's segmentation. Purchasing professionals have their own analysis tools to determine which few suppliers are worthy of strategic investment, and it is as few as 5 per cent in some cases. A simple split between strategic business relationships and tactical sales was a reasonable first step for the new world. The chemicals company Dow responded assertively to this trend in 2002, spinning off bulk sales of commodity chemicals and silicones to an e-business-only subsidiary. Despite worries on Wall Street at the time, this move soon proved its worth.

So far, so good. With a substantial body of literature to inform the relationship-oriented approach to strategic accounts, and even more about the

[1]The Industrial Marketing and Purchasing Group is an informal international network of academics whose research is focused on the interface between marketing and purchasing in business markets. It was established in the 1970s and continues to generate theory about the dynamics of business relationships. For more information visit **www.impgroup.org**

potential of user-friendly portals, the new-style sales management was on its way. However, some further challenges remain under explored. Account managers often ask about the distinction between 'key' accounts, where strategic intent is clearly mutual, and 'keep' accounts, where the customer sends confusing signals, such as 'We want your expertise, but you must get the price down' or 'You are our preferred supplier, but we are still going to use your competitors'. If a customer's market position or purchasing policy suggests that they are not treating a supplier strategically, the supplier has to withdraw resource, transparently and constructively, without losing business that is keeping the factory running. Win-win negotiating skills are critical here, but we find much of the research that helps with 'keep' accounts in the fields of general strategy or even law. The cataclysm of the breakdown of major business relationships is also difficult territory; proactive risk reduction and exit strategies are worthy of more study.

On a more encouraging note, after masses of publications about the profitable retention of customers, a few papers are emerging on the dynamics of acquiring new customers. Concern about the way mergers can undermine shareholder value has triggered new interest in 'organic' growth. It is where the interplay between marketing and sales, a current hot topic for researchers, has fascinating potential.

EXPERT VOICE

PART D

DIRECTOR'S TOOLKIT

In Part B we introduced ten core tools and techniques that can be used from day one in your new role as a team leader or manager in your chosen field. As you progress up the career ladder to the role of senior manager, and as your team matures in terms of their understanding and capabilities, you will want to introduce more advanced or sophisticated techniques.

Part D provides a number of more advanced techniques developed and adopted by industry leaders – helping you to differentiate yourself from your competitors.

	TOOL DESCRIPTION
T1	Team sales management audit
T2	Coaching tick sheet
T3	Key account planner
T4	Sales campaign summary sheet

T1 TEAM SALES MANAGEMENT AUDIT

How do you know if your team is maximising its potential to sell? Use the following checklist to assess the current state of your team. Consider each criterion in turn and use the following scoring system to identify current performance:

0 Not done or defined within the business: unaware of its importance to sales management

1 Aware of area but little or no work done

2 Recognised as an area of importance and some work done in this area

3 Area clearly defined and work done in the area in terms of managing sales

4 Consistent use of best practice tools and techniques in this area across the business

5 Area is recognised as being 'best in class' and could be a reference area for best practice

Reflect on the lowest scores and identify those areas that are critical to success and flag them as status Red, requiring immediate attention. Then identify those areas that you are concerned about and flag those as status Amber, implying areas of risk that need to be monitored closely. Status Green implies you are happy with the current state.

ID	CATEGORY	EVALUATION CRITERIA	SCORE	STATUS
S1	**Salesperson – right people**		0–5	RAG
A	Performance	You measure their activity, knowledge and skills, not just their output		
B	Induction	You have an induction process and a clear development plan for all your salespeople		
C	Selection	You have an objective and demanding process for choosing new salespeople – you do not just use 'gut feel'		
S2	**Sales pipeline**			
A	Selection criteria	You have clear, consistent and well communicated selection criteria for prospects and customers at different stages in the sales process		
B	Long-term value	You judge customers on their lifetime potential value, not just the current business they give you		
C	Conversion ratios	There is a measure of conversion ratios at each stage in the sales process and you are aware of what influences those ratios		
S3	**Market trends**			
A	Monitoring	You have a process to monitor and check the latest trends and best practice in sales		
B	Competitors	You spend an appropriate amount of time monitoring and checking what your competitors are doing and what unique selling propositions they offer		
C	SWOT	You and your team carry out regular SWOT analyses and take action based on them		

ID	CATEGORY	EVALUATION CRITERIA	SCORE	STATUS
S4	**Sales planning**		0–5	RAG
A	Forecasts	You know how many suspects, prospects, customers and key accounts you need to meet your targets	☐	☐
B	Effort and time management	The resources you provide to sell and service individual customers is proportional to the long-term value they bring your company	☐	☐
C	Monthly cycle	There is a detailed activity plan one month ahead and a high-level activity plan three months ahead	☐	☐
S5	**Momentum**			
A	Maintaining customer interest	There is a way to maintain customer interest and move the sales process forward between sales visits	☐	☐
B	Passing customers on	There is a clear plan for when responsibility of a customer is passed from one salesperson to another and the customer sees the transfer as positive	☐	☐
C	Stalled progress	You are able to identify when a sales process has stalled and can identify what action is required; this should include a Go/No Go decision	☐	☐
S6	**Sales process**			
A	Defined	You have a clearly defined process to ensure you are interacting with suspects, prospects, customers and key accounts in the appropriate manner and are constantly moving the process towards an agreed goal	☐	☐
B	Tools	Your salespeople use common and consistent tools at different parts of the sales process and you use technology to assist	☐	☐
C	Skills	You know what knowledge and skills are required at each stage of the sales process and you have a system to apply the best resources at each stage, or improve competence levels if you do not have the ability to select different people at different stages	☐	☐

ID	CATEGORY	EVALUATION CRITERIA	SCORE	STATUS
S7	**Key account management**		0–5	RAG
A	Defined	You have a clearly defined method to agree which customers are key accounts (this goes beyond total spend or total volume)		
B	Approach	Key accounts are treated in a significantly different way from your standard customers		
C	Communication	All customer-facing staff are aware of who are your key accounts, why they have been chosen and how they should be treated		
S8	**Salesperson – right skills**			
A	Measure	You have a method for objectively measuring individual sales people's skills and knowledge on a regular basis		
B	Building capabilities	You use a combination of coaching and training to get staff up to an agreed standard of knowledge and skills		
C	Motivation	You have a system to ensure your staff are motivated to develop their knowledge and skills		
S9	**Customer focused**			
A	Empowerment	All your staff are empowered to make the right decisions when faced with a customer question or issue		
B	Long-term value	Your relationship with customers is based on the long-term value you provide the customer, not the short-term revenue that you can earn from them		
C	Customer relationship management	You have a system to ensure all staff have the appropriate knowledge of a customer, their relationship with your company, recent transactions and their value to you; and that system automatically does not require duplication of effort by the customer		

ID	CATEGORY	EVALUATION CRITERIA	SCORE	STATUS
S10	Salesperson – right results		0–5	RAG
A	Where sales are coming from	You know where your results over the upcoming period are coming from: key accounts, regular customers and prospects; this also requires knowledge of customer churn	☐	☐
B	Contingencies	You have contingency plans in place for the loss of strategic customers and staff, and you have an effective risk and issue management process	☐	☐
C	Mix and monitoring	You have the right mix of customers in each segment to optimise revenue and profit, and your monitoring process is not too tight or too loose	☐	☐

For each element of the checklist add up the scores of the three related questions and divide by 3 – this will give you an average score for that specific element. Here is an example:

ELEMENT	SCORE	0	1	2	3	4	5	NOTES
Salesperson – right people	2.2			■				We do not measure anything except results
Sales pipeline	4					■		Our people constantly canvass
Market trends	2.6			■				We do SWOT analyses but do not know enough about the current competitive position
Sales planning	4					■		Although somewhat by chance, we put the right effort into the right places
Momentum	1		■					Too many prospects stay on the list for a long time before removal

ELEMENT	SCORE	0	1	2	3	4	5	NOTES
Sales process	2.9				■			There is more than one process in use
Key account management	1.6		■					There is no real system in place for this
Salesperson – right skills	2.6				■			We recruit intuitively and lack a training culture for salespeople
Customer focused	3.1				■			Our CRM system is not reliably up to date
Salesperson – right results	4.2					■		We are getting good results that could be better if we had a proper key account management system

In an integrated sales management framework the whole system is only as good as an individual element. If one 'link in the chain' is weak, then the integrated sales framework within the company will not operate to optimum efficiency and there is increased risk of failure. Your action plan, therefore, should be to focus attention and resources on the elements of greatest weakness first, and then to move the whole framework to a level of excellence. This approach optimises the use of resources and sets up a process of continuous improvement.

In the example above, the *momentum* element (average score 1) and the *key account management* element (average 1.6) are the weakest links and are the priority areas to address. Once you are confident that these issues have been resolved, the next stage would be to focus on the areas in Amber.

T2 COACHING TICK SHEET

There is no better place to coach than when you are out with a member of your selling team. If you use a consistent checklist, salespeople will improve their performance. Here is an example for the absolutely key discovery meeting. Use it or adapt it to meet your own requirements.

Discovery meeting checklist

Where 1 equals poor and 9 equals excellent, mark the performance of a salesperson on this checklist:

POOR	SCORE	EXCELLENT
Weak introduction	1 2 3 4 5 6 7 8 9	Strong, personal introduction
No explanation of purpose	1 2 3 4 5 6 7 8 9	Clear purpose of meeting
No motivation of customer	1 2 3 4 5 6 7 8 9	Motivates customer
Uses closed question too early	1 2 3 4 5 6 7 8 9	Starts questioning with open questions
Does not listen	1 2 3 4 5 6 7 8 9	Listens and uses what they have heard
Moves from subject to subject	1 2 3 4 5 6 7 8 9	Logical and well organised structure of questions
Customer is in control	1 2 3 4 5 6 7 8 9	Salesperson is fully in control
Salesperson makes assumptions	1 2 3 4 5 6 7 8 9	Salesperson makes no assumptions
Discussion is awkward	1 2 3 4 5 6 7 8 9	Discussion flows and is informative

POOR	SCORE	EXCELLENT
Negative, 'cold' climate	1 2 3 4 5 6 7 8 9	Positive, 'warm' climate
Salesperson presents too early	1 2 3 4 5 6 7 8 9	Salesperson withholds presentation
No summary	1 2 3 4 5 6 7 8 9	Accurate clear summary
Summary ignores customer's language	1 2 3 4 5 6 7 8 9	Summary uses customer's language
No checking question used at end of summary	1 2 3 4 5 6 7 8 9	There is good agreement as to what has happened
No next steps agreed	1 2 3 4 5 6 7 8 9	Next steps agreed

T3 KEY ACCOUNT PLANNER

Many industries continue to become more concentrated, which means that they are becoming dominated by a smaller number of larger customers. Under such operating conditions, the effective management of those accounts becomes critical to survival and success.

Use this key account planning tool as part of an annual planning process for your most important customers. Use it to challenge how well you really understand their business, your relative strengths and weaknesses and ultimately your readiness for success.

CUSTOMER PROFILE	
Customer name	What is the name of the external or internal customer that this account plan covers?
Primary purpose	What is the customer's mission statement or purpose: a short statement of the customer's overall aim? Note: think about what would be missing if they no longer existed.
Products and services	What are the customer's main products and services?
Markets and customers	What are the customer's main markets and who are their customers?
Unique capabilities	What is unique or special about this particular customer in terms of what they do for their customers? Why do their customers choose to use or buy from them as opposed to other providers?
Positioning and brand	How does this customer position themselves with their customers? Note: think about what their 'brand' stands for and what their operating principles are.

Core processes	What are the customer's core processes? Note: identify activities that are critical to the effective supply of their products and services to their target customers.
Structure and people	How is the customer's team structured or organised and how many people are employed?
Geographic locations	Where is the customer located and where are key decisions made?
Funding, growth and profitability	How is this customer funded and what is their performance in terms of revenues, budgets and contribution?
Customer strengths and weaknesses	What are the key things that will help the customer to achieve their mission and what are the main bottlenecks? Note: reflect on the customer's products, services, customers and markets, and on the current operational capabilities.
Impact	What is the impact of these strengths and weaknesses? Use a simple scale of H = High, M = Medium and L = Low.
Customer opportunities and threats	What are the key things that will help the customer to achieve their mission? Note: reflect on changes in the customer's operating environment, such as regulations, technology, economic conditions or competitive threats.
Impact	What is the impact of these opportunities and threats? Use a simple scale of H = High, M = Medium and L = Low.

ACCOUNT OBJECTIVES

Objectives	What are your key objectives for this customer? Note: all objectives should be SMART: S = specific M = measurable A = agreed R = realistic T = time-bound
Priority	What is the relative priority of each objective? Note: reflect on which will have the greatest impact on your performance and that of your customer.
Indicator	What will be the end result or deliverable once each objective has been achieved? How will you know if you have succeeded?
Timing	What is the expected date for completion of each objective?

Status	What is the current status in terms of meeting each objective? Use a simple colour scale: Red = major concerns and corrective action is required. Amber = some risks and needs to be monitored carefully. Green = on track and should be complete within the target time frame. Black = completed.
Our strengths and weaknesses	What are the key things that will help you to achieve your objectives with this customer and what are the main bottlenecks? Note: reflect on the your products, services, customers and markets, and on the current operational capabilities.
Impact	What is the impact of these strengths and weaknesses on your ability to deliver? Use a simple scale of H = High, M = Medium and L = Low.
Your opportunities and threats	What are the main changes in the way the customer operates that will affect how you meet you objectives? Note: reflect on the customer profile and assess how they might be changing in the light of their opportunities and threats.
Impact	What is the impact of these opportunities and threats in terms or your ability to meet your objectives? Use a simple scale of H = High, M = Medium and L = Low.

READINESS AUDIT

Account readiness	What is the status of this account in terms of performance against each readiness item?
1 Level of contact	Have we got the right level of contact within the right customer team? Note: this should include key stakeholders and decision makers.
2 Reputation and brand	Does the customer currently view our business, team and 'brand' in a positive light?
3 Customer understanding	Do we understand enough about the customer's strategy and operations to be able to complete a thorough customer SWOT analysis?
4 Customer musts and wants	Do we understand why they seek to work with suppliers – what are the customer's musts and wants?
5 Strategic products and markets	Are our products and services strategic to the customer? Note: consider whether we address key activities in the customer's operating processes.

6 Operational excellence	Can we provide the necessary products and services in an effective and efficient manner?
7 Competitive performance	Are we best suited to provide selected products and services to this customer? Note: we might be highly efficient but if we price ourselves too high, or a competitive provider (internal or external) does a better job, then we risk losing this account.
8 Future opportunities	Have we identified specific opportunities for future development and growth?
Score	What is the current score? Use a 10-point scale, where 0 = no progress at all and 10 = ideal performance.

Status	What is the current status for each item?
	Use a simple colour scale:
	    Red = major concerns and corrective action is required.
	    Amber = some risks and needs to be monitored carefully.
	    Green = on track and should be complete within the target time frame.
	    Black = completed.

Resource requirements	What additional resources will be required to manage this account successfully?
Budget	What additional (non-operational) budget will be required for each item?

Status	What is the current status of each resource type?
	Use a simple colour scale:
	    Red = major concerns and corrective action is required.
	    Amber = some risks and needs to be monitored carefully.
	    Green = on track and should be complete within the target time frame.
	    Black = completed.

T4 SALES CAMPAIGN SUMMARY SHEET

Here is a simple way of defining how well your sales campaign is going. The sales process can take various lengths of time. When selling consumer goods you can aim to close the sale at the first meeting. In complex sales where a number of people are in both the selling team and the buying team it can take a lot longer, up to six months or more. But in essence the milestones in the process are the same.

Summarising the position

A campaign summary sheet records your progress in the sale. It takes the form of a radar diagram showing your level of success in eight essential areas.

1 Customer need – measures the impact and urgency of the customer's requirement.

2 Finance – records if the customer can justify the purchase and has money available to buy it.

3 Key people – checks how easy it is for the salesperson to meet all the key people.

4 Timescale – records when the customer is likely to buy.

5 Solution – measures how well the supplier's products and services meet the customer's need.

6 Basis of decision – shows how well the salesperson can meet the customer's buying criteria.

7 Practicality – necessary with complex products to show how practical it will be for the customer to implement your solution.

8 Competitive position – reminds you that you have to persuade the customer not only to buy, but also to buy from you rather than anyone else.

Take this summary sheet to each sales call as an aide-memoire. As you go through the sales process, measure your performance in the eight areas by scoring them on a scale of 1–10. The areas that remain weak, the low numbers, are the areas your sales activities must address. When all the items score at or near 10 the customer will be ready to buy.

Here is an example of a radar diagram that shows graphically the situation you are in now:

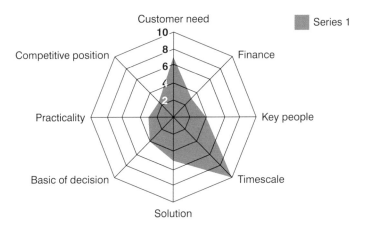

It is clear from this picture that the salesperson has a good understanding of a real customer need. Whether or not the finance is available is in doubt. The salesperson knows some of the key people but there is work to be done there. The timescale is fine – the customer plainly realises that they have to act and soon. The solution the salesperson is proposing needs some more work. The salesperson has not defined the whole basis of decision that the customer is using. In terms of practicality there is no agreed implementation plan. Finally, the competitive position is not as good as it will need to be if the sale is to be made.

As you go through the campaign, updating this picture will ensure that you are putting effort into the right areas.

THE FAST TRACK WAY

Take time to reflect

Within the Fast Track series, we cover a lot of ground quickly. Depending on your current role, company or situation, some ideas will be more relevant than others. Go back to your individual and team audits and reflect on the 'gaps' you have identified, and then take time to review each of the top ten tools and techniques and list of technologies.

Next steps

Based on this review, you will identify many ideas about how to improve your performance, but look before you leap: take time to plan your next steps carefully. Rushing into action is rarely the best way to progress unless you are facing a crisis. Think carefully about your own personal career development and that of your team. Identify a starting place and consider what would have a significant impact on performance and be easy to implement. Then make a simple to-do list with timings for completion.

Staying ahead

Finally, the fact that you have taken time to read and think hard about the ideas presented here suggests that you are already a professional in your chosen discipline. However, all areas of business leadership are changing rapidly and you need to take steps to stay ahead as a leader in your field. Take time to log in to the Fast Track web-resource, at **www.Fast-Track-Me.com**, and join a community of like-minded professionals.

Good luck!

OTHER TITLES IN THE FAST TRACK SERIES

This title is one of many in the Fast Track series that you may be interested in exploring. Whilst each title works as a standalone solution, together they provide a comprehensive cross-functional approach that creates a common business language and structure. The series includes titles on the following:

→ Strategy

→ Innovation

→ Project management

→ Finance

→ Marketing

GLOSSARY

ABC account classification A classification of customers by potential spend

accompanied visit A joint meeting with a manager, colleague or trainer and A salesperson and a customer

account Another name for a customer

account executive Performs the same or more senior role as a salesperson

account manager A sales representative normally responsible for key or national accounts

account representative Performs the same role as a sales representative

action plan Stated tasks, deadlines and responsibilities to achieve an objective

active listening A listening skill used to capture the real meaning of what is being said, capturing insight and strategic words

aptitude Natural ability to perform an action or task

assertive selling A type of selling used with prospects with significant spend where you have little or no existing business

awareness A marketing measure of how many or what percentage of target customers are aware of a particular product or brand

base customers Customers who tend to be large and not very profitable, but who reduce the cost of providing a product or service through economies of scale

benefit An attribute of a product or service expressed in terms of the positive impact it has on the user

benefits The advantages gained from a product or service

brand A name, design or features that distinguish one product or company from another; the brand is often associated with perceptions and perceived benefits

budget An estimate of sales and costs in providing the product or service, often set annually

business case A formal analysis of a new idea to validate whether it will provide a satisfactory return on the investment required to make it happen

business-to-business [B2B] Commercial transactions between two organisations which do not involve sales directly to consumers

business-to-consumer (B2C) Commercial transactions between an organisation and the consumer which do not go through a third-party channel

churn The loss of customers or staff

client Another name for a customer

closing Gaining commitment from a customer to purchase a product or service

coaching To train someone to improve their skills level through showing, briefing, observing and debriefing

cold customers Either a prospect or a lapsed buying customer

consumer The user of a product or service; this may or may not be the person who buys it

contribution The gross revenue less variable costs (also called contribution to fixed costs)

contribution to fixed costs The gross revenue less variable costs

cross selling Selling additional products or services to existing customers

customer The person who purchases a product or service

customer needs Specific problems to be solved by a customer

customer penetration ratio The percentage a customer spends on your products and services against the total the customer could spend on your products and services

customer relationship management (CRM) A system that captures and displays a history of all interactions your company has had with its customers

daily sales plan A day-to-day plan of a salesperson's sales calls, listing who will be contacted, how they will be contacted, whether they are prospects, buying customers or key accounts, and the objectives of each call

decision-making influencers People who have an indirect control over the purchasing decision

decision-making people People who have a direct control over the purchasing decision

decision-making process The steps taken to make purchasing decisions

decision-making unit The group of people who make purchasing decisions

differentiation The distinct attributes or features of an idea, product or service that help to provide a source of advantage over competitors

elevator pitch A statement that explains in less than 30 seconds what you and your company does and leaves the listener wanting to hear more (see also *positioning statement*)

fear The concern that something may go wrong

features Characteristics of an idea, product or service that provide benefits to customers or consumers

first impression The opinion made about someone or something in the first few moments

funnel Often used to refer to the shape of a graph when starting with prospects and moving to key customers, taking into account the conversion ratios at each stage of the sales process

gate keeper A person who is in between you and a decision maker or influencer and who has the power to permit or restrict access

hard sell A pushy sales approach that does not allow the customer to make a purchase decision of their own free will

hiring Employing new staff

hook A piece of information about a customer or prospect that will allow a salesperson to connect more quickly

information Data; often a salesperson will obtain this in the early part of the sales process to establish needs, wants and requirements

insight More powerful than information, in that it goes beyond data and may enable a salesperson to come up with a more easily differentiated solution

key account A customer who is of strategic importance and requires to be treated in a different way from normal customers

lapsed buying customer A customer who has not purchased a product or service for a preset (agreed) period

margin Gross profit divided by sales revenue

market price A price set by demand and supply pressures for a specific product or service

market share The sales of a particular product, service or firm as a percentage of the overall market

mission statement A concise explanation of how we will achieve our goals

motivation The willingness to perform

negotiation The process which takes place when a buyer's need to buy is equal to the seller's need to sell

network A group of people that you maintain contact with, normally having common social and business interests

networking Using your network for the exchange of information and support

no names policy When a company will not divulge any details of its employees; normally they will ask you to write to a department and wait for a response.

objection A resistance in the form of a statement or reason offered to the salesperson by the buyer

one to ones Meetings (normally face to face) between managers and their reports to discuss results, activity and knowledge, and skills development

opportunity A potential sale yet to be qualified

perception What customers, competitors and staff think of your company and your brand

positioning statement Also referred to as an elevator pitch, a summary of what you and your company do and a statement of how your company is perceived by your target market

price points A series of prices that will generate a certain demand; companies often set a number of price points for salespeople to use for different sized orders

products Goods or services created and sold to customers

product development The process for developing a new product or service from initial concept or idea to in-market commercialisation

product life cycle The stages that a new product will go through: introduction, growth, maturity and decline

prospecting The process of identifying suspects and prospects who have the potential to buy your product or service

prospects Suspects that have been through a selection process and are worthy of a sales resource being dedicated to them

references Examples of effective solutions you have delivered to buying customers that you can give to prospects in order to demonstrate credibility

referral A prospect that is given by a current customer or prospect

requirements The customer's needs and wants which the product or service could fulfil

salesperson A catch-all description for anyone involved in sales, either office-based or field-based

sales process A series of steps sales-people follow, from choosing a suspect through to development of a key customer

sales representative A salesperson, often a representative of a company, responsible for maintaining good customer relationships

segmentation The process of divid-ing a large market into smaller groups; each sub-group will have similar characteristics and will therefore simplify the process of analysis and targeting

sleeping customer See *lapsed buying customers*

soft sell When the sales process follows a natural flow and is not perceived by the customer or prospect as being 'pushy'

stretched target A higher target to motivate the sales team, often not published outside the sales group

suspect A potential customer who has not been researched and has only passed through basic selection criteria

SWOT analysis An assessment of an idea, product or market using four criteria: strengths, weaknesses, opportunities and threats

target market The group of customers or consumers that is most likely to buy the product, or that represents the most significant strategic potential

target An internal goal, often higher than the company budget; this can also be set (or flexed) more fre-quently than the budget

telemarketing Calling prospects or suspects by phone to qualify or 'warm' them up

telesales Selling on the telephone rather than face to face

tools Templates, reference points, spreadsheets and checklists to aid the sales process

transactional selling A selling approach where the product or service being sold is identical to all the competitors

up selling Getting customers to buy more expensive products or services

unique selling point (USP) The element of your product or service that your competitors cannot offer

value added The result of adding or combining features to a product or service in order to increase the overall worth

value added selling A selling approach that demonstrates tangible value for the customer in the business relationship

value proposition A simple statement that describes the value a product or service gives to the customer or consumer; the word 'value' implies that it will describe benefits (possibly measured in financial terms) and not features or attributes

value statement A framework of behaviours you expect the employees to follow

vision A view of the future state of the business: what it could be if everything went according to plan

vision statement The company goals that are communicated both internally and externally

voice of the customer (VOC) An understanding of the musts and wants of different customer or consumer groups and the relevance to the organisation and individual teams

warm customer A customer that is going to be receptive to your personal approach

warm up A process where you start the customer interaction before you make a personal approach; this could be by email, letter, web newsletters or articles that you or you company have had published

WIIFM 'What's in it for me?' – always think what the customer will get out of any interaction

INDEX

Page numbers in **bold** relate to entries in the Glossary.